Nuns With Nightsticks

By

David Michael O'Rielly

To my Grandparents, Antonio and Adelina, for their brave hearts in coming to America to raise an exceptional family.

All my aunts and uncles who showed me what family means in living with respect and honor. Thanks to my parents in heaven, who are looking down now thinking you really were literal. Oops sorry.

Acknowledgment

The person who guided me, encouraged me, and had faith in me is my wife, Jackie.

I would never have finished this without her. Thanks to the project manager, James, and Maria, the editor, for helping me at every step of the process of publishing this book.

Table of Contents

Chapter 1

Childhood Adventures In The Holy Land Of Ithaca Street

1960

I was born in the Holy Land and spent a lot of time in Galilee. I would roam the city streets and visit marketplaces, shops, and cafes with my parents. Just imagine walking on the same streets and steps as Jesus.

Wide-eyed, I took it all in, watching tourists rushing into the shops. They would bump into each other, pushing their way into crowded displays of things to purchase for their families back home.

Some would try and negotiate a lower price, to no avail. A few shops would display a guest book for tourists to sign, and you could see all the places they came from. It was amazing to hear all the different accents in every shop we entered.

I would be unable to see everything in the small shops due to the number of people blocking areas where things could be seen and bought. People just standing there, deciding which item to purchase for a memory of the Holy Land. It would upset the people who were waiting behind them. They would fidget and mumble comments, looking around the shop.

My parents would go to the guest book first and sign us in so our names would be in each store we visited. Sometimes, we would turn the pages back in the guest books to see our names from the last time we were there. In the book, you put your name and address, and you wonder if you recognize anyone as you glance over the pages.

I found it difficult to navigate the streets as it was easy to get lost. I could not see over the people to know where I was. People would come out of the shops with bags of trinkets and shirts with "Galilee" on the front or back as memories from the Holy Land. Baseball caps were becoming popular, and I wanted one to wear it proudly.

One time, when I had a cap in my hand to purchase, dad took it away from me and put it back on the rack. He looked down and whispered, "We are not tourists, so there is no need to buy something with the name Galilee on it."

I can still smell the food from the street vendors and various restaurants with difficult names to pronounce. With certain smells coming from the marketplace, I had an idea where I was at any given time. Only the heat of the day could slow us down, so our family would then find some shade for us to rest and eat.

Galilee was even more of a wonder watching the men casting nets to catch giant fish that would be taken to the processing plants. When they towed the nets, they would catch bottom fish like cod, haddock, flounder, red hake, and whiting.

When the wind would pick up, the foul smell of fish would encase the town and make it unbearable to walk the streets. I was in awe of them as they worked on small boats and worked in perfect harmony throughout the day. There were so many boats with names painted on the back and sides.

I would watch them leave in the morning and return in the afternoon with boxes full of ice and fish. Walking around at sunset on the shoreline, taking in the end of the day with tired, sore legs from a day of adventure.

Surely, I felt like the luckiest kid in the world as I imagined seeing the Apostles in every face I met. I was blessed, to say the least, and my face glowed in the Holy Land.

The letters on the crucifix, INRI, inspired me as I delved into a rich history of the Catholic faith. I was only five years old, but I had the faith of a child and searched for answers. I could not get enough answers, and my questions would flow from my lips, usually sucking on candy cigarettes.

Everywhere I looked, I would see other children playing and wondered if they felt the same as me. Do they realize how cool it is to live in the Holy Land?

I knew what INRI meant on top of the crucifix; it was simple to figure out. I didn't have to ask anyone what the letters meant. Everybody knew what they meant.

When in church, I would look up at the crucifix and realize I am blessed to live in the Holy Land. To know that Jesus Loves me and, in a way was my neighbor.

INRI means 'In Rhode Island', where Jesus lived. I knew this to be true, and do you know what? I had proof of this. I lived in Warwick, Rhode Island, and the distance from our home to Narragansett was just 24 miles. Within Narragansett, there are two fishing villages called Galilee and Jerusalem!

You now see just how easy it was for me to know that I lived in the Holy Land. It took a long time for me to realize that I may have been mistaken.

INRI is the Latin phrase "Jesus Nazarenus Rex Iudaeorum," meaning "Jesus of Nazareth, King of the Jews."

Right now, I need to explain myself to you about my affliction, and to this day, I still do not have a cure. It has embarrassed me all these years, with people giving me strange looks, laughing, and making fun of me. My belief in INRI was just the beginning, and it only got worse as I got older.

You see, the affliction is being too literal-minded. The definition is understanding words and statements only in the most basic and ordinary way and not having much imagination.

As I tell you my story, you will understand all that has happened one step at a time. So, get ready for this literal journey I am taking you on. You will be reading history on diverse levels. Yes, I, at times, interpret what other people say based on the actual meaning of the words. I process the information differently than most people.

I do encounter misunderstandings and confusion from other people. This may not be a hindrance, as I turn it around into humor. If you are unable to laugh at yourself, then you are not living a Literal Life.

My mother was FBI, which, as you know, stands for Full-Blooded Italian. My father was English and Scotch-Irish, or as they say, British Isle. They had what you called in the day a mixed marriage. Irish and Italians had their differences, and there were so many that confusion became a normal way of growing up.

My parents purchased a home in Warwick, Rhode Island, on Ithaca Street, right off Sandy Lane. Before this, we lived in the city of Providence.

So, being the product of a mixed marriage had its challenges, to say the least. My parents had different ideas on how to raise their family of two girls and a boy. I was the middle child, my mother's favorite.

No, seriously, just ask my sisters; they will tell you the same thing.

I was premature and spent over a week in an incubator. I was sickly when I was a toddler, and mom and I had a special bond over this. Due to my shriveled-looking body, my nickname was 'Little Chicken'.

I looked more like a raisin with arms and legs. I would spit out the nasty-tasting medicine, and mom would have to run me down and corner me to get it in my mouth. It sure did work as I grew into my sausage fingers, making this story difficult to type.

The one thing my parents believed was this: we will not educate our children. My dad said the Nuns are education experts. They will keep the kids in line to focus on proper education. This was my dad's idea. It was a bad idea, and I am here to prove it.

Here you go; here is a perfect example of this. I did not go to kindergarten and had to fend for myself to learn about the world. Again, there are no Nuns in Kindergarten, so no school. I did not know my birth date, street address, or phone number. My parents did not even teach me how to count or the alphabet to learn the letters that form words.

Nuns were the answer when it came to educating their children. I had no idea, being clueless. I was a walking enigma. I did not even realize that I needed to know these things. Can you believe this?

I was born on Easter Sunday, and even to this day, we celebrate my birthday on Easter. Every Easter, I would get up early in the morning. In the beginning, I was in a crib begging my parents to get a real bed! I had to sleep in the fetal position because my feet would hang out of the bars in the jail cell that they put me in.

Anyway, I would climb out, walk down the hallway, and yell to high heaven, "I have risen! I have risen!"

I would then hear my dad scream out, "Blasphemy!"

To be honest, I still say it today. It's kind of a tradition with me.

On Easter, I would play outside with a new toy that I could show my friends and say, "Look what I got for Easter!"

This would make me feel special, as my parents went the extra mile to provide gifts on such a great holiday. However, in time, they realized it was also my birthday, so I was no longer special.

Many of my friends received more and the most popular toys for birthdays and Christmas. It was very noticeable, and I never said exactly what I received. I figured we were just a poor family, and it was best not to think too much of it. One good toy was enough for me.

One of the best toys for Christmas in 1960 was The Alamo Soldiers Set. This was an excellent gift for me as I already had the Davy Crockett coonskin hat and a suede leather-fringed jacket to wear while playing, thanks to my older cousins who lived next door.

This was not a new Alamo set; it was from one of my cousins, purchased years earlier, and was not cheap like the new sets. But it was new to me, and that was all that mattered.

He even had some of the small soldiers in a bag. The problems with the set were the colors of the fort were fading, and the walls would not attach to each other. They would crash on the non-carpeted floor. My solution was to put several of my shoes behind the walls to fix the problem.

My older sister got a twirling baton for her cheerleading. My little sister received a baby doll. When my little sister would leave the room, I used to take the doll's head off. She would start screaming when she saw the head a few feet from the body. Then I would walk back in, head held high, reattach it, and be the hero. She fell for that every time. What are big brothers for?

On Christmas Eve, we would go to the old Italian Social Club in Cranston. All the kids would gather around the white aluminum Christmas tree filled with large colored lights and huge red velvet balls.

People we didn't even know would hand out toys we could play with while visiting. They would come and go, so we received a lot of toys. I must admit, they were not expensive toys but toys to play with while waiting.

One of my aunts would come in with a large bag filled with toys just for us. My head would be spinning around and around, looking at all the toys under the beautiful tree.

The next stop on our Christmas Eve adventure was visiting four of our Italian families' homes and receiving more toys. We would eat Italian cookies and ribbon candy. My cheeks would hurt from my aunts squeezing them and telling me what a good boy I was. I am telling you, it really did hurt.

On Christmas, we stayed home alone as a family. This was our special time. We would attend church first, then return to open all the gifts, and then we put them into our rooms.

We only played with our toys in our rooms. This way, the home was not cluttered and messy all day and every day. We had family rules to live by, and this was one of them.

My parents were frugal and looked to save money wherever they could. Our 52 Chevy still had clear plastic on the front and rear seats from when the car was purchased.

New cars all had plastic on the seats. The furniture in the living room had clear plastic on it as well. We only sat in the living room when the company came. Otherwise, we would be in the kitchen, the meeting place for the family, or just playing in our rooms.

I liked hanging out under the kitchen table as I had more room to play using my imagination. I would be in all kinds of fantasy hero stories.

Mom would make cinnamon twirls with leftover dough, and her hand would come down below the table for a good treat. There were times when my legs were in the way, so I would have to stop playing and sit in a chair with everyone else. I pretended that under the table was my fort, my world of fantasy.

Ithaca Street was an ideal place to raise a family back in the 50s and 60s. Starter homes with families that all knew each other. These homes were built around 1951.

My dad's sister lived next door. She was one of my dad's favorite siblings and looked like the mother who starred in 'Father Knows Best'.

She was like a second mother to me as she watched us when mom had to go to work. She was the only family on my dad's side that we knew well.

Living next door to the family was like a warm embrace. It was comfort and security all in one. The boys were about seven to ten years older than me, so I did not play with anyone next door. But in a young neighborhood of starter homes, there were plenty of kids around of all ages.

On Friday or Saturday night, there would be a party at someone's home, and the parents would get together for a night out without the kids. By doing this, they all saved money, and it was 'BYOB' or bring your own booze.

The party areas would be in the basements of each home to keep the noise down for the young kids sleeping upstairs. We had a bar in the basement with a dance area along with a record player.

This was great because we would have a babysitter named Cheryl. She was the IT girl for me. I was in love with her.

How could I not be? She had blonde hair and blue eyes. She was so cute that I could not get her out of my mind. She looked a lot like Haley Mills. Anything she asked me to do, I did it with glee.

She was my first love, but this lasted only a few months. This one time, I was peeking out the window of my room, facing the street. There was Cheryl, kissing and an older boy right on the front steps. She had a boyfriend already! I was heartbroken. I had to move on, as they say. I realized she was an older woman of thirteen, too old for me.

But younger girls all had cooties, so I had to put my love on hold. Of course, I did have a huge crush on Annette Funicello from the Mickey

Mouse Club. She looked like one of my cousins. I did not care about anyone on the show but her.

She passed away two days before my birthday in 2013, and I just had to think of how I felt back in the day. I needed to smell some Play-Doh for comfort, but I had none.

I wonder why no one has ever made a fragrance with the smell of Play-Doh.

Our neighborhood had a gang from five years old to sixteen. We would hang out daily in small groups, only meeting together as one group when needed.

On December 12, we ended up with a snowstorm of 10.6 inches. Two days later, the streets were again covered in fresh new snow, and light flurries were sticking to the street. At the end of the street, barriers of plowed snow were held, piled high up, way over my head.

It was cold so I was wearing a heavy coat and mittens, you know, without fingers. I was stomping around in my black galoshes when some older kids came up and dared me to do something I had no clue about

I had never talked on the telephone; like I said, I did not even know our home phone number. The only phones I knew about were two cans and a string saying only "hello" back and forth. After a while, the can would hurt your ear.

18

Has it happened to you, too, huh?

The older kids dared me to climb up on the snow mound and pull down the lever on the telephone pole. It was a huge mound, but I knew I could climb it. After all, it was a dare!

"That doesn't look like a telephone!" I yelled back at them.

"It is a new kind of phone," they responded. "It is an outside phone, that's why it looks different. Just pull that lever down like we told you to. Start talking when you pull it down."

I looked around, and all the kids were looking right at me, yelling, "Come on and do it."

I must take the dare; there is no way around it. I was being challenged. They are older, and I wanted to impress them with the idea that I could do anything. I wanted to fit in and be accepted. I yelled back that I would do it and started climbing Mount Everest!

I pulled the lever down, saying, "Hello, hello?" but no one was on the line.

It was not a phone; how could this be? You mean these kids lied? Why would they have me do this in the first place? I thought we were all friends.

One kid yelled, "You're in trouble now; the fire truck will show up, and you will go to jail for pulling the fire alarm!"

Another kid yelled, saying, "It is a silent alarm, and a special powder is now on your mitten, only visible with a flashlight."

I looked down and did not see powder on my mitten. I guess they were right; the powder did not show up.

I carefully climbed down the snow mound. Each second, I could feel my heart beating like a base drum and just as loud. When I got to the street, I looked around, seeing a circle of faces laughing at me. It was me who pulled the fire alarm.

Voices were yelling at me, "They will find you! They will find you!"

My face was now hot, with sweat dripping down my face. I had to get out of there, but I was frozen solid with fear.

Then one of the kids yelled, "I hear the fire truck, and it is coming here. Run, run for your life!"

They ran off, leaving me alone, standing still, frozen on the ground.

Why are my legs not moving? I had to think and think fast. What should I do? Shaking with fear, thinking oh, I am going to get it good when dad gets home.

They will find me!

Chapter 2

Adventures Of A Little Menace

You have never seen little feet move as fast as I did that day. The friction from my corduroy pants felt like sparks were igniting and were hot. I thought my pants would catch fire. You could hear the fabric swishing like the breeze from down the street.

I ran into the house out of breath, and my mom knew I was in trouble. I did not bother cleaning or taking off my four-buckle boots or jacket. Anyway, I was crying and could not stop. I was unable to make any words come out of my mouth – just a good screaming and sobbing noise.

My mother looked down and kept asking, "What is wrong? What is wrong?"

Do you know the saying, hiding behind your mother's skirt? Hell, yeah, and damn proud of it too. I was sitting on the floor, shaking in my snow boots, with a puddle of water surrounding me from the melting snow. It seemed like forever, but a heavy, loud knock at the back door made me scream and holler even more. They had found me! They had found me!

Three firefighters were on the back steps. My mom went to the door, and I sat behind her, protecting the rear flank. Each one of them took turns to tell me what a bad kid I was to pull the fire alarm. Pulling the alarm is not a game to be played.

They could see me sitting on the floor behind her wide-eyed and thinking when dad gets home, I am going to get it. This meant the belt, as my mom's weapon of choice was the wooden spoon. Either way, kiss my ass goodbye. I knew what that meant.

The firefighters decided to instill the fear of God in me so I would never do it again. I was losing it; my tears were flowing like Niagara Falls. At that time, I just wished I was wearing my Davy Crockett coon skin cap at the time to provide me with a little courage or my two six-shooter cap guns so I could shoot my way out of this trouble. Dad is going to whip me a good one.

Then, my mother spoke in a tone I had never heard before. Mother bear was now my protector. She pulled the door wider, then took a few steps closer, leaving me in the open with no cover! I was unprotected in the middle of the kitchen. With only a stern mother's voice, she looked them dead in the eyes, enough to shame Gary Cooper in High Noon.

"You have said enough! My son understands what he did was wrong. You have made this point perfectly clear. But I will ask you one thing: why is the snow piled up so high next to the telephone poles? My 5-year-old son was able to climb it?"

The big guy in front said, "Well, Ma'am."

"Enough! Get off my steps and leave my son alone!" Mom yelled, slamming the door shut better than George Jefferson.

I was still crying, knowing I was going to get it good from the belt – the weapon of choice for my father. I was wondering which belt he would use. I pondered that for a moment.

Pulling me straight up, mom said, "It is over; stop crying."

"I can't," I stammered, "Dad will come home and spank me good."

Mom wiped the tears off my face and said, "Your father does not have to know about this, and it will be our secret. You have learned your lesson today."

My mom walked a lot taller that day. Mom became my hero!

One note here: a few years later, my nickname from the parents in the neighborhood was David the Menace. I always wondered why my parents put me to bed every night by 7 pm. My dad said I could not watch Dennis the Menace because I might get ideas, so 7 pm was the deadline.

Are you kidding me? In the summer, it was still light outside. What is up with that? When I watched the reruns, I knew he did the right thing.

My first practical joke was probably not a good idea. I just turned five, and Joanne, my sister, was three. We were in my room playing, and I had an idea to play a joke on mom.

I told Joanne to lie down and pretend to be dead. I asked her not to move until I said so. Joanne always followed my lead. After all, I was her big brother.

I entered the kitchen with my arms waving and screaming. "Mom, Joanne fell down, and she is not moving!"

I sure was a good actor. Mom raced to my room and called out Joanne's name twice, but she did not move at all. My sister was a trooper.

Just then, I said, "Okay, Joanne!" She raised her head and started laughing. I was laughing, and my mom was relieved.

Mom then explained how this was not funny and how it scared her. At the same time, she made sure my butt knew the severity of the bad joke I had played. Joanne got off because she was only three.

Mom penalized me, and I could not watch *Mighty Mouse*, my hero. My dad spanked me when he got home, and like he always said, "You're getting this for good measure."

What does that mean? Thinking he was paying it forward for the next time, I did something wrong. Shouldn't I be paid ahead by now!

Nuns With Nightsticks

When I was around three years old, my mom would tie me to the backyard clothesline. This way she could do the house cleaning and cooking and not be interrupted by you know who. By doing this, I had a range to walk about 10 feet in any direction. She did this to prevent me from trying to ride my tricycle up to Sandy Lane.

Once, she had to chase me down the main road because I was about 3 feet from Sandy Lane. She was pregnant with Joanne at the time. Boy, could she run fast!

I was always on the move. I would just take off and explore. I understood her reasoning for tying me up. I was okay with it at the time and played with my toys by myself. But when we got a dog named Toby, mom tied him up on the clothesline, too!

At first, I was jealous of Toby, but it was then that I realized I was being treated like a dog! No other kid on our street was tied up on the clothesline, just Little Ol' Me!

I was in the backyard playing, and a hornet got inside my zipped-up light jacket. The single hornet stung me three times, and I ran around in circles, screaming. I panicked and did not think to unzip the jacket and let the hornet out.

Suddenly, mom threw me to the ground and unzipped my jacket so the hornet could escape. She told me what to do if this should ever happen again. Once more mom came to my rescue!

25

Dad called a family meeting. These were never good and mostly about us going somewhere and not acting up and causing embarrassment to the family. We always practiced manners at the table again and again if we had to visit someone. You know, sit up straight, hold your fork properly, stop kicking your sister.

To this day, I am surprised I do not have a dent or a sore spot on the back of my head. I always sat next to dad for easier reach. Our family meetings were always centered at the kitchen table, and dad would stand up and give us a presentation. I wondered what was going on now.

"OKAY! Against my better judgment, your mom and I have decided to get a dog." Dad announced.

I almost fell out of my chair! We all yelled sounds of pure joy. I did not know any cuss words in English to properly explain my glee at this age, only in Italian. Since mom knew Italian, I had to keep my mouth shut. She thought I was probably an angel. At least, I assumed she did.

We spent the next few minutes voting on a name for the dog. Of course, dad yelled out the first name, and we ended up deciding on his choice. He suggested the name Toby. I objected; that name was rigged as we really did not have a choice in the name. However, dad later admitted that the dog already had the name Toby, and we would keep it the same. At least I got him to admit it.

That's one small step for a kid – one giant leap for kid kind.

Nuns With Nightsticks

We only had Toby for a few months because dad kept him outside, and he would not stop barking. Toby was a brown, 35-pound, short-haired dog that was very energetic and loved to play.

I told dad he would not bark in the house if he stayed in my room. But dad said no, the dog stays outside. With constant complaints of Toby's barking, we had to give him to a farm, or so I was told.

This broke my heart as I missed Toby. He had become my best friend and dog confidant. Dad said we could visit Toby, and I asked to see him several times. But we never went, and after a while, Toby became a distant memory.

Instead, Joanne and I decided to play with mom's fox fur. We treated it as if it were a dog and threw it all over the house. Mom finally caught us and said some words in Italian that I had never heard before. With her tone of voice, I don't want to hear them again.

Also, mom said dad was allergic to dogs, which is why Toby could not stay in the house. I wondered why they did not tell me that in the beginning. Of course, she had to explain what an allergy meant, and it took some time for me to figure that one out.

So that is why he sneezes so much, I thought. He would sneeze ten to twenty times in a row, and we kids would yell out the number of sneezes, and in between the numbers ten or eleven, he would yell out, "Shut up, you damn kids!"

David Michael O'Rielly

I was a red-headed kid with freckles and a crew cut. I wore a black high-top 'Keds' sneakers with jeans rolled up at the bottom. I wore a t-shirt with the left side sleeve turned up and over, holding my box of candy cigarettes. This is how we rolled back then—always wearing a Boston Red Sox ball cap.

In my back right pocket would be my pocketknife. In the left back pocket were baseball cards with which to trade or gamble. I was just a smooth guy ready for anything.

When I got on my dad's nerves, he would say, "Go play in traffic."

The first time he told me this, I went outside to play in the middle of the street. I got into trouble due to blocking cars coming up and down the street. It would take a few moments to pick up my army men.

Dad was alerted by people honking their horns. He came out onto the street and pulled me into the house. When he asked why I was playing in the street, I looked up and said, "Dad, you told me to play in traffic, so I did what you told me to do!"

Then there was this other time when he said, "Go play far, far, away."

I asked him how far that is, and he said, "Very far, far, away."

I got it and crossed the horse track behind our house. I kept going until I could no longer see the neighborhood. When I came home for lunch, I got in trouble for not answering the call to come home. Mom usually just opened the back door and yelled, "David!"

This time, I was over an hour late for lunch. For some reason, my stomach did not notify me it was time for lunch.

"Dad, you told me to play far, far, away, and I did, so why am I in trouble?" I asked innocently.

He then replied with one of his favorite expressions, "Jesus, Mary and Joseph!"

During this time, we went to my Italian grandparents' house every Saturday. They lived in Providence on Hendrick Street in the Mount Pleasant neighborhood. This was less than a mile and a half from Atwells Avenue on Federal Hill. A small white two-story house, 876 square feet, built in 1930.

All the aunts in the family would come and clean the house and visit with my grandparents. The women in the kitchen were loud and boisterous with laughter. English and Italian words were being spoken with hands waving all over the place to ensure their words were well received. It was like listening to a song by Louis Prima called. "Angelina."

Many of them had the same name, Mary, an extremely popular name for girls over the years. With all the Mary names, if you wanted to distinguish which Mary you were talking about, it would be like this: "Joe's Mary is going to the store" or "Steve's Mary might be going along."

For a kid, this was very confusing.

Many of my aunts did not drive a car or have driver's licenses. The uncles would do all the driving when needed. In Providence, you could take the bus to go shopping.

Riding a bus was commonplace back then, like when my dad was on the bus heading to mom's house. This was his first time picking her up on a date and meeting my grandparents.

He was sitting there and locked eyes with a fellow passenger. They were both wearing the exact same ties, nodding that it was a good choice in fashion. When the stop came, my dad got off the bus, and the guy with the same tie also got off. They walked down the sidewalk together, realizing they were going to the same house. The other guy was one of my uncles.

The small kitchen is where all the women would congregate after cleaning the house. It had a potbelly stove and a regular stove to boot. A red and white kitchen table with a belly drawer that contained silverware.

Across from the kitchen was the butler pantry. There were glass door cabinets filled with dishes and plates. A bread container to keep the

Italian bread from getting stale was on the counter. When the kids were growing up, they would eat 11 loaves of Italian bread a week.

At the end of this was the bathroom under the stairs, with a toilet and sink; that was it. The ceiling sloped over the toilet, so there was no room for a shower or tub. The boys were washed in the butler pantry, and the girls were washed in the bathroom sink.

I would sit in a rocking chair by the potbelly stove, watching all the hands waving in amazement, all the while wondering what they were saying.

There would be four or five conversations going on at the same time. So, I would pick one and listen, attempting to understand as best as I could. I could understand most of the English words and a few Italian words. When Italian and English were used in the same sentences, I would get confused about what was being said.

Understand that my grandparents had 11 children, and with married-in aunts, this place would be jumping. Keep in mind my mother was the second youngest out of 11 children. This meant I had cousins who were over twenty years older than me.

In fact, my grandfather was born in 1882, and my grandmother in 1886. My oldest uncle was born in 1904. My grandpa came to the United States in 1899 from Galluccio, Italy, and my grandmother arrived in 1900 from Teano, Italy.

31

They met on Federal Hill, falling in love. In time, they purchased their home on Hendrick Street. My grandfather was a Wool Comber for forty-seven years and retired in 1947.

Whenever I visited my grandparents' house, I was drawn to the rocking chair I absolutely loved. As soon as I arrived at my grandparents' house, my sole purpose would be to spend time rocking in that chair. At some point, I would drive everyone insane from so much rocking.

I would rock the chair back and forth so fast I would almost launch myself across the room. This would be the signal that I had to leave and stay with grandpa in the living room and hopefully take a nap like that was going to happen.

Dad always said I had ants in my pants. But I did not feel them crawling on me.

I could not totally understand the words coming out of my grandpa's mouth. People would call it broken English. He was 5 foot 11 and weighed 200 lbs. He had huge forearms, and he always wore gray work pants with a white undershirt, a tank top, and an unbuttoned short-sleeve collar shirt over this.

The way grandpa would look at you was something special. He made you feel like you were the best thing in his life. He was always explaining things to me and asked a lot of questions. We would watch

The Lone Ranger and other Western movies and talk during the shows. On top of the TV was a ceramic black panther.

During the shows, you would hear hawkers (street vendors) yelling in the street, selling produce, saying, "Fresh strawberries, fresh strawberries!"

No nap for me, not with grandpa around. I perfected my hand, speaking to the point of perfection. Grandpa and I could speak by hand! It was the only way to communicate. I should have been a symphony conductor.

About twenty-five years earlier, my grandfather wanted to tell his boss what a great guy he was, but he did not know proper English to speak to him. He asked some other Italians standing around what to say in English. After learning what to say and practicing the words, he went up to his boss and put his arm around him.

He said something like, "Hey Boss, you a real nice son of a bitch."

When my grandfather returned home later that day, he made one announcement. "English is to be spoken from now on in this house!"

Now, being from an Italian household, my grandparents had one rule. When you get married, you must live in their house for one year to learn how to be married. My grandfather was the head of the household, and you did not purchase a car or home without his permission.

My dad said, "I am Irish, and no Italian is going to tell me what to do!"

Right, tell that to mom; go ahead, I dare you. In all fairness to dad, my grandparents treated him like a redheaded stepchild. I figured it was because he had red hair.

Chapter 3
From Grandma's Kitchen To Childhood Adventures

My grandmother was a great cook and would serve everyone first before she would sit at the table. Grandma was 5 foot 2 and weighed 200 lbs, the same weight as grandpa. I found her weight on her application filed with the Alien Registration Division.

Grandma never became a US citizen. I heard it was because she was always taking care of children and the ten kids next door when the parents went to work.

When the mother passed away, the obituary mentioned that all the girls were named Mary. Grandma was 'Mama' to all who knew her. She looked after those kids for years.

One time at lunch, she was passing out bananas and gave my uncle a larger piece of banana than my aunt. My aunt asked grandma why she got the smaller piece, and she replied, "Ah, Tony was in the war, dear, so he gets a bigger piece."

My little sister would cause my grandmother to rant, rave, and talk Italian so fast she would be beside herself. You see, my grandmother made the best pasta fagioli, and other Italian soups. There would be Italian cold cuts like the olive loaf, but that was awful for a kid.

"Gimme that mortadella please!"

But my little sister would have none of it. Joanne wanted peanut butter on Italian bread and eat it upside down. This way, her tongue would taste the peanut butter first. It kind of made sense to me.

Joanne would smack her lips, unable to close her mouth while eating. Grandma would shake her head, mumbling in Italian, and go back to her station at the stove.

Joanne also had another issue. None of her food could touch each other. If it did, she would not eat what was placed in front of her.

Grandma did not understand this but complied with her wishes. My dad told Joanne that the food all went in the same place and came out in the same place, explaining that the food touched each other. Joanne didn't buy into that—no way, now how?

One time, when my cousin Steven was sick with a fever, my grandmother put a ring of raw garlic bulbs around his neck to heal his cold or flu-like symptoms. He said the smell was bad enough to yell out, "I'm healed!" But there was a more practical way of healing.

Removing the curse of The Evil Eye, commonly known as il Malocchio', was taught by my grandmother to Martina, the eldest daughter. This is taught to someone only on the night of a full moon. The Evil Eye is given to another person because they desire what the other person has. It is a look one gives to another or the way one feels about someone. The curse can cause physical pain or misfortune.

The trained person is called a 'Strega', an Italian Witch. To remove the curse, you must have olive oil, holy water, a silver dish, salt, and scissors. The Strega or someone else pours the olive oil into the holy water inside the silver dish. If it takes the shape of an eye, then the person is cursed.

You do not need to be a genuine Strega to perform this. But it is cool to have a Witch do it. You know what I mean?

The process is this. Use the scissors to cut the air over the dish, and make the sign of the cross three times. Then, you place your hands on the person affected. Then say the following:

"Father, this prayer is being said for (insert name), and I pray it works in the name of the Father, the Son, and the Holy Ghost (Spirit now). Repeat the following three times. Say one, Our Father, One Hail Mary, and One Glory be."

If the curse has not been removed, then this must be performed only with the Strega. The same steps listed above, but you recite the following in addition:

David Michael O'Rielly

Envy and the Evil Eye

Keep your horns within your eyesight.

Death to envy, and may the Evil Eye explode.

In the name of God and Holy Mary, may the Evil Eye go away!

Holy Monday, Holy Tuesday, Holy Wednesday, Holy Thursday,

Holy Friday, Holy Saturday, and the Evil Eye dies on Easter Sunday!

I always wondered why they did not just say every day of the week. Then, pour salt in the water, perform the sign of the cross three times, cut the water with scissors, dump out the dish, and repeat these steps three more times. Now, to protect from future Evil Eye curses, you can do the following: Tie a red ribbon over the threshold of the home. Then, throw salt out all the doors to protect from envious people.

Do I believe in the 'Evil Eye'?

Yes, and I have the Italian Horn (Cornicello) tattooed on my leg for protection. By having the Cornicello and the word Malocchio that is tattooed on my arm I am constantly reminded not to be envious of others. Be happy with what I have like when I was a little boy.

On many weekends, I would spend the night with my cousin Steven in the city. They lived over the TV repair shop they owned on Mount

Pleasant Avenue. Every night I stayed there, I would hear a thump, thump, thump.

Finally, I asked Steven what this was. He said cars were running over manhole covers in the middle of the street.

After that, I could sleep soundly to the noise, which eased me into sleep. Just like the foghorns going off at Point Judith in Narragansett when I would stay with them at the beach house.

Many times, two of my uncles would come by grandpa's house and take me for the day. They were married into the family. Thomas and Richie were best friends. They were the ones who taught me how to count and talk with my hands, and it came naturally to me. Counting would be like the number 1, which would be your thumb, and your pinky, which would be 5. Remember this as it goes into Nun lore about this later.

We would go to the clubs in Cranston and Providence. Just imagine a little five-year-old walking into a bar. They would pick out an old guy to keep me occupied and sometimes play checkers with me.

Thomas would say, "Hey kid, we got some business over in this other room. You stay here and stay out of trouble."

After thirty minutes to an hour, we would go to the next place. Basically, I was their cover.

They used to take my older cousin before me and my older sister before him. It was an adventure, and I got to meet a lot of adults who really liked my uncles. I was treated very well when I had to wait for them. I played a lot of checkers or tic-tack-toe when I went to each place.

I became a little Thomas and Richie, walking and talking the same way with hand speech. Richie reminded me of Frank Sinatra, and Thomas reminded me of nobody, really. He had a round face and body and was a wisecracker big time. All the time, he was playing jokes with me and others. He would tell a story as only a Sicilian could.

Our family was from Galluccio, Italy, about 35 miles north of Naples, high up the mountain on the edge of the extinct volcano Roccamonfina. Years later, I went to see the family in Galluccio and realized just how special my family was.

Family is everything, and living a simple life with respect and honor is important. Your success is measured by the smile on your face and the smile of those who you know.

Many tourists from America make derogatory comments about the difference in Italian food and how it is prepared. They would comment on how Italian American food was better. I would say this is an arrogant position as you are in a foreign country and should treat this country with respect. To learn its ways and people to get a good understanding of the culture you are experiencing.

Nuns With Nightsticks

In Italy, you do not get served a plate or bowl of olive oil to dip your bread into unless they know you are from America, and then they will make exceptions. Pizza is not covered in sauce and meat, and with dough so thick, you are now eating a pie. The pizza is thin with sauce, a little cheese, and some meat or anchovies.

I simply explained that in Italy, people walk daily running errands. Food is prepared, so it is not in excess to where you gain weight. Small portions with several courses if so desired. The menus are several pages, with each page having a first course, then a second, and so on.

I did not see a lot of overweight Italians in Rome or elsewhere. Seasonal fruits and vegetables are used for meals in each season. You have never tasted tomatoes like the area around Naples, which is so full of flavor, or the large lemons in Sorrento.

Growing fruits and vegetables is different than in America due to the volcanic soil, so fertilizer is unnecessary. Simple traditional meals have not been reinvented, except in high-class restaurants.

I grew up eating more traditional Italian food. Grandpa had a lovely garden, and grandma showed the girls in the family how to prepare a well-balanced meal with fruits and vegetables. Mom carried on this tradition. I learned the old ways of things in my short life.

David Michael O'Rielly

My extended family were my teachers in life. Learning from observation and how people react to situations and conduct themselves. I was watching a movie in real life every day.

One time Uncle Richie took my older cousin Steven, who was like an older brother, and I fishing on some breakwaters. This is a large pile of rocks built parallel to the shore. It is designed to block the waves and the surf to provide calm water for harbors.

We walked down to go on the rocks with rods, reels, and one tackle box. I was behind my Uncle Richie and noticed he had a pistol in his jacket pocket.

I said, "Uncle Richie, why do you have a gun in your pocket?"

He told me, "Land sharks, kid, Land sharks."

I then looked over at the shore for land sharks walking on the sand.

Ritchie yelled, "Kid, what are you looking at?"

"I am looking for land sharks walking on the sand. Do they just come out of the water like that?"

Years later, I found out there were problems on Federal Hill. Interesting time around the Office, also known as the Coin-O-Matic Vending Machine Company. I made up the family names in case it came back to haunt me. It would be easier if I didn't have to make up names, but some folks might get offended.

Nuns With Nightsticks

Uncle Richie would take me to a salt pond, and we would dig for quahogs. I would use the clam rake, and Uncle Richie would use his toes to dig down and feel the hard shell of the quahogs.

The large quahogs are used in clam chowder or with linguine. Another way is steamed and served with a lot of friends with Narragansett beer and corn on the cob with drawn butter.

In a restaurant, you would ask for littlenecks (smaller clams) served raw on an open half shell. I liked them better, steamed and dipped in butter. I like the stuffed clams called 'Stuffies'. Back in the day, you had shacks along the coast that would sell fried clam cakes. They would have chunks of clams inside served in grease-stained paper bags.

Now, the clams are minced with a slight clam flavor. I go to Iggy's when I am in South County, which is the best around. Some might even say George's restaurant in Galilee.

I must say this: when it comes to clam chowder, the Rhode Island clear broth style is the best. You get chunks of quahog clams in every bite. Some people prefer the New England style with cream. The problem here is the richness of the cream, and you do not get enough clams. I do not care for Manhattan clam chowder, and I am not the only one.

Cookbook author and Chef James Beard had this to say about this soup.

"That rather horrendous soup called Manhattan clam chowder resembles a vegetable soup that accidentally had some clams dumped into it."

He got that right, for sure. If you like clams, Rhode Island clear broth is what you order.

I was baptized at St. Rita's church in Warwick. Once in church, I passed out because I had no air conditioning. I woke up on the front lawn of the church with a Police Officer giving me smelling salts. He and I then sat in the patrol car until mass was over. I remember asking many questions, and he always repeated the same answer.

"What's this?" I would ask.

"Don't touch that."

Over and over until I knew what everything was in the patrol car. I went to turn on the siren so the cherry light on top of the car would go off, and he quickly grabbed my hand.

"Listen, kid; we do not need to scare everyone in the church, so hands off."

"Yes, sir! But can't we just try it for a second?"

In time, I would be ready to go to Catholic School at Saint Kevin's on Sandy Lane. This was within walking distance of our home. I did not want to go to school as I was having fun at home. Behind our home and behind the fence was a quarter-horse training track with a lot of tall grass surrounding the track.

As kids, we would go out to the field and get close to the horses, and they would chase us back to the fence. It was scary at first, but the horses liked us. I got over being scared when I heard that one of the horses bit off a kid's arm two houses up from me. I was told that his arm had grown back to normal. With this tidbit of information, I could run out to the field without any worries.

We used to set traps in the field to make kids fall when the horses were chasing us. We would tie the tall grass together with two hands by twisting the grass, making a nice-sized opening where you could get your foot caught in it.

When someone was running, they would get their feet caught in the trap and fall. It was great fun scaring others. For hours, we would sit on top of the fence, taking it all in, imagining riding a horse and playing cowboys with a white hat against a black hat.

I had a pop gun and would put corks in the barrel and shoot cans off the top of the fence. Other times, I would knock the cans off with my slingshot. Of course, I always had my two cap guns ready.

During this time, I went to the hospital quite often. One time, I was playing with my toys in the backyard. This older kid from up the street came and played with me. I wondered why this kid, who was easily five or six years older, would want to play with me.

We got into an argument, and he picked up a shovel and hit me on the head. When I got out of the hospital, I was told his family would be moving out of the neighborhood. Apparently, the kid had some major issues. Word had it that his mom was having an affair with the milkman. I wondered what my head had to do with it.

One day, my dad and I were driving in Providence. Years later I found out what really happened. Dad hit the brakes hard, and of course, we did not use lap belts in the 1952 Chevy, and my forehead hit the metal dashboard.

Turns out my dad confessed he was looking at a woman out the side window. When he faced the front, he had to brake hard so he would not hit the car in front of him. Back to the hospital for stitches.

In the summertime, they would take the horses down to Little Pond on West Shore Road, and the horses would go in for a dip. They would take most of the dirt off with water and then brush the horses. After that, we were allowed to go swimming in the pond. This was the only area with a beach big enough to walk down and enter the water from our side of the pond.

This is how I learned to swim. The mothers would sit in lawn chairs and teach us how to swim, starting at the shoreline, and every year, you went out a little deeper with the mothers yelling out swimming instructions. The pond had an area of black sludge, and when your feet landed on it, it felt squishy. It was nasty and smelly, and it just so happened there was a drainage pipe feeding the pond right in the middle of the dark water.

Every time we came out of the water, you had to stand next to your mom so they could inspect your body and pull the leeches off your backs, arms, and legs. It was all I knew and seemed normal to me. Doesn't everyone have leaches taken off when they go swimming in a pond?

Little Pond was a great place to fish as well as swim. In fact, at one end of the pond, there was a school called Veterans High School that backed up to the pond and had a good-sized sandy beach. I would fish for catfish called hornpout or mud cat in some country areas. They were brown bullhead fish and liked to eat leeches, which was okay with me.

Hornpout fish find their prey by taste and smell using their sensitive barbels or whiskers. They have three venomous spines on their pectoral and dorsal fins. If you pick up the fish improperly, you will feel the pain of the protective fins, and your hand will go numb.

This was why I always carried a towel to handle the fish. I had a red and white pole with a small metal tackle box. I used the night crawlers and would dig up each day I went fishing.

David Michael O'Rielly

One time, I caught some frogs and wanted to show my mom. I grabbed a bucket and collected quite a few. On the way back to the house, I had to bop them on their heads to keep them in the bucket so they would not jump out. I put the bucket down and ran into the house to get mom to come outside to see my frogs.

When I went out to get the bucket, it was empty. My mouth was wide open in amazement. Mom had a good laugh at that one. She had to explain that they jumped out and hopped away. Next time, put something over the bucket to keep them from jumping out. Just a smooth guy ready for anything.

Joanne and I would walk along Little Pond, and I told her the story that was told to me. Dragonflies, also known as the devil's darning needle or, as we knew it, as sewing needles, were something to fear. It was said that if you tell a lie, they will sew your lips together.

So, after her first walk with me along the shoreline, the next time, we asked each other if we had recently lied. If we had, we had to keep our mouths wide open and walk as fast as possible.

By the pond was a little hill where we made a small cave and kept a couple of candles in it. Of course, we did not carry matches, so we would mostly sit in the dark. But we had the right idea to begin with. It did not last long after some older kids found it. They jumped on top of it and caved it in. We really worked hard on that cave, and now it is gone.

We just found another place to hang out. This was my tree-climbing time, where I would catch the frogs. It was what I was telling you about when we went swimming. It was right by the drainage pipe with the smelly water. I loved climbing trees and would try to get close to the top as I could then go to a lower, sturdier branch to sit on.

Kids would walk by, and we would call out for them, but they would be unable to find us. They never looked up to see where we were. I thought I should be a ventriloquist.

Chapter 4
Growing Up In New England

In school, we studied about the Indians and how they saved the Pilgrims during the first winter. They showed them how to raise corn, beans, and squash. The trick was to remove the topsoil and deposit fish that would turn into fertilizer. I already knew this, as Uncle Richie told me what to do with the fish I catch. I guess living in, New England, we studied this time period thoroughly.

Side notes: If you ever get the chance, go to Plymouth, Massachusetts. You'll go back in time to see how the settlers and Indians lived. The Indians lived a much better life in wigwams than the Pilgrims did. The Pilgrim homes were of 800 square feet with hard-packed dirt floors and a thatched roof, all in one room. The designs were typical English cottage homes. I just thought about my dad snoring with us all in one room—no sleep for anyone.

The tale of relocating Plymouth Rock for preservation is quite remarkable. In 1774, a team attempted to haul Plymouth Rock from the shore and put it in the Town Square. However, it broke in two. The bottom half was left embedded on the shoreline, while the top half moved to the Town Square.

In 1834, the rock was moved again to the front lawn of the Pilgrim Museum. Unfortunately, the rock fell from the cart and broke in two once more. A small iron fence was used to keep souvenir seekers from using hammers and chisels.

A Victorian-style canopy was constructed in the 1860s to cover the lower portion of the rock that remained embedded into the shoreline. In 1880, the rock was returned to the harbor and reunited with the base. The date "1620" was carved on the stone's surface.

Now, Plymouth Rock is perhaps half the original size due to breaking twice and the damage from hammers and chisels by souvenir seekers. Only a third of this rock is now visible today, with the rest of it under the sand. You can even see the cement that was used to piece the rock together.

I must admit, it was small, and I felt cheated, unable to see the original rock in all its glory. I couldn't help but laugh when I saw the cement holding the rock together.

In the spring, mom decided she wanted to plant flowers between the bushes in the front of the house. Thinking I could help with the fertilizer, I took on the task. It took me two days to catch six hornpouts. Without telling mom what I was planning to do, I removed the topsoil and put the whole fish where mom was planning to plant, just like Uncle Richie had instructed me to do. I was such a big help.

A day or so later, mom went out front with a tray of flowers to plant. As she dug up a little dirt, she hit something unusual. She reached down and pulled out a full hornpout. I heard her scream, "Why is there a fish in here!" Then she found another one, then another. At the top of her lungs, she yelled, "David!"

Realizing my mistake, I had to remove all the fish. So, I took them back to the pond for turtle food, as they are scavengers. Apparently, mom did not know about using fish as fertilizer.

Once, after getting the belt, I was very upset and mad at my father. I went to see a neighbor, Mick, a friend of mine. He was a great guy, and we got along very well. We liked to do the same things and even dressed alike. He was shorter than me and had blond hair.

Mick knew more about things than I did. He was a man of the world. Not a short man, just a kid. He knew a lot of stuff a literal guy like me would be clueless about.

We decided to run away that evening. He was to come to the house and get me with a signal. Of course, we forgot to figure out what the signal would be—a minor detail on our part.

As it turns out, dad and I were on the mend. During our family dinner, we were all laughing, and I forgot about wanting to run away.

So, Mick came to the back door by the kitchen. He started throwing small rocks at the door every few seconds.

Dad asked, "What was that?"

I quickly responded, "I didn't hear anything?"

Mick threw the rocks again, and now I did not know what to do.

"What is that hitting the back door?" Dad asked once more.

Again, I responded quickly, "I did not hear anything. Did you hear anything, Joanne?"

"Nope, sure didn't. What was I supposed to hear?" she replied.

I knew I had to tell Mick I had changed my mind and that dad and I were on good terms again. I went to the back door and quickly told Mick I was staying home and that everything was okay now. My dad could overhear what was being said and that I was happy now.

Mick decided to run away anyway, went past the horse track, and hid until he got too hungry and scared and went home. He had an adventure, and I was jealous and wished I was with him.

I remember at supper time, we would have the radio on and listen to music. Sometimes, we'd even stop eating to sing along to a song. One of our favorite songs was by Hank Williams.

Back then, when we went to someone's house, you didn't knock on the back door or ring the doorbell. Instead, you'd raise your voice and say in a sing-song way, "Hey, Miiick? Hey, Miiick?"

Each morning, I would go over to Mick's house to get a second bowl of cereal. One time, he was eating slowly, and we had things to do. We always had plans.

I said, "Mick, pick up your bowl and drink the milk and cereal. Forget about the spoon. I do it every morning, and you should do it too."

Mick picked up the bowl and downed it. His mother overheard this and gave me some real words about manners and not eating like a pig.

"David, you are no longer allowed to come here for breakfast. You are a bad influence on Mick," she declared.

I replied, "But it is easier to eat the cereal this way if you are in a hurry."

She looked down at me and said, "Both of you leave right now."

No more second breakfasts for me. That really sucked.

In the winter, we would ice skate and look out for ice holes used for fishing. These holes were big enough that you could fall right in. One house on the pond had a few ice holes for fishing, and we stayed away from this area. In fact, a friend of mine became a celebrity when he skated dead-on toward the opening in one of the ice holes and fell right in.

I asked him how it happened. He said he did not know how to stop or turn when skating on the double blades. As a result, he went toward that opening like a moth to a flame.

We had this baseball field on top of the hill overlooking the pond. As little kids, we would take our sleds and go down the hill on hard-packed snow, then onto the ice for another 20 feet. Older kids would stand on both sides of the hard-packed snow. Then, when we went down the hill, they would jump on top of us, knocking the air out of us so we could go a lot further than sledding alone. We always tried to go down the hill as fast as possible so the older kids would fall off.

I fondly remember taking wax candles and rubbing them on the sled runners for more speed. Not so fond memories of getting the air knocked out of me. I thought at the time it was keeping me skinny, so it was worth it.

The neighbor across the street was the same kid who fell in the ice hole. His dad was a State Trooper, and he made the most impressive snow fort you could imagine. I wondered if he was on the TV show "Highway Patrol" with Broderick Crawford, but I never saw him on the show. He was a hero to all the kids in the neighborhood.

The older kids made a fort opposite his fort, but it was nowhere near the quality. We divided the kids between the two forts to have a great snowball fight. The big and little kids teamed up, making it a memorable night.

I was in the smaller fort, and we lost when the fort fell apart due to the shoddy way it was built. We got overrun with snowballs flying all over the place, and guys were jumping over, smashing into the walls.

During this time, my sister Mary and my cousin Ann came to watch from the back steps of our house, witnessing the war of the century. A couple of the older kids were messing with Mary, teasing her and throwing snowballs at her. At the time, I didn't know they were flirting; I thought they were trying to hurt her.

I ran up to our leader, who was easily five years older than me and started to hit him. I got a few punches in before he threw me to the ground. He then told everyone to nail me with snowballs. At least six kids started pelting me. I retreated to the back steps and ended up in the fetal position to protect my face.

The back door flew open, and mom yelled, "What is going on here? Stop this right now and leave."

Mary later explained to me that the leader of our gang liked her. It was not a big deal; they were just playing around. She thanked me for coming to her defense and trying to help her. She patted me on the head and asked if I was alright. I felt good after this.

Mom came to the rescue, and it turned out the leader liked my sister. I thought to myself, "I got it made! I got it made!"

One time, our family returned from church, and piles of snow were everywhere. By the back steps, the snow was piled up higher than the steps. When they got in the house and started taking off their boots and coats, my mom asked where I was.

I walking up the steps and fell straight down in the snow mound. No one knew what happened to me until they heard me yelling for help.

I mentioned earlier that we were in a gang. We had a leader who had a couple of friends to keep the rest of us in line. Once, we went to a house with a huge rhubarb garden. I had been there before with Mick on one of our adventures and ended up eating so much rhubarb my lips swelled up.

Now, we were by the red two-story house meeting in the rhubarb garden. The older kids decided we were going to break into the house. The house was across Sandy Lane, opposite the horse track. My friend Mick and I would be the lookouts and stay at each end of the house, far enough away to signal if the cops were coming.

I hoped we would be together at the same end of the house. We were supposed to whistle if we saw the cops, but there was one problem. I forgot to tell anyone I did not know how to whistle. I was too embarrassed because Mick could, but now he would be on the other end of the house.

What was I to do?

We all left, planning to return in a couple of hours. Mick and I hung out in the field with the horse track since we did not know how to tell the time; at least, I didn't. Now, I was worried, hoping I would not have to whistle.

Mick and I went to plan our escape if we had to run from the cops. We went out in the field and set the grass traps, a bunch of them, to stop anyone from chasing us. Then we went to the house to be the lookouts.

About 15 minutes after the kids entered the house, a cop car came down my side of the street, slowly coming towards the house. I tried to whistle, but nothing came out, just air. I had to yell and yell, which scared everyone in the house. Kids jumped out of windows and ran through the front and back doors. Everyone ended up screaming and yelling.

Mick and I hooked up and ran to the field where we knew we would be safe. However, we made one critical mistake while setting the traps. We did not lay out a safe pathway through the traps; we had set them randomly. We ran with both of us, getting our feet stuck in the traps, getting up, running, and falling again, scared to death that we would be caught. The cops caught a few of the older kids. Not much happened after that.

After this incident, I was not used as a lookout until I could whistle loud enough for the next time I might be needed. It seemed like I practiced forever, at least that summer. "You know how to whistle, don't you, Steve?" as Lauren Bacall said in 'To Have and Have Not'.

The answer was, "Hell no, pretty lady, I do not!

My previous job was when I just turned five years old. I was small enough to break into small basement windows, go through the house, and unlock the back door for an older kid to enter the home. It was hard to get to the floor without hurting myself; I had to look for a bench or chair to land on.

One time, someone had seen me break a window and climb though. Now, I was in the hot seat. I became an actor that day worthy of an Academy Award! In other words, when dad grilled me on this, I played the angelic child and denied everything. I convinced my dad it had to be another kid. I offered up no one and was prepared to face the consequences myself.

Because of this, I became a lookout but ended up screwing that up as well. It seemed like crime was much harder than I thought it would be.

Back then, when we played cops and robbers, no one wanted to be a cop. I had a toy Tommy gun and felt like a winner with this in my hands. We all wanted to be the bad guys. Only in westerns did we like the good guys because they always won.

When Chubby Checker came out with the song "The Twist," it was a huge hit, and everyone was dancing to it. People would even use the hula hoop to get in shape for this dance. At wedding receptions, you would do the Limbo Dance and then dance the Twist. It was funny seeing some of the adults do the Twist. Wedding receptions were always fun, except I had to wear a suit and tie. Luckily, I used a clip-on tie that would easily come off when Limbo started.

My older sister took it upon herself to get me ready for school. She told me about the Nuns and what they were like. She said they have eyes in the back of their heads and can see and hear everything in the classroom. I was terrified, as now I knew what it meant when someone said, "Hey, four eyes!" Two sets of eyes seemed like such an advantage, and I only had one set; what a disadvantage I had. I mean, they could see things coming and going!

St. Kevin's Parish was established in 1956, and Father Raymond Murphy was the first priest. The school was built in 1958 and opened in 1959, and I entered in 1961. The Nuns back then would wear the full habits. What is a habit, you might ask? Well, it is a little complicated, but here you go. Imagine if you had to wear all this and wear it on a high-temperature school day.

The Tunic is the central piece of the habit, a loose dress made of serge fabric pleated at the neck and draped to the ground. My sister said you never see their legs or feet, and she was right! It was like they were walking on air. The Scapular is the symbolic apron that hangs both front and back and is worn over the Tunic and tied under the belt.

The Coif is the garment headpiece and includes a white cotton cap secured by a bandeau and a white wimple to cover the neck and cheeks. A guimpe to cover the chest of starched linen or cotton covered by a thin layer of black crepe. The Veil is worn pinned over the Coif head coverings.

In other words, a Full-habit Nun wore more clothes like armor than the Knights in the Crusades and were tougher than the Knights, I'll tell you!

I am just five years old and soon going into first grade to face the horrors of the Nuns. My sister ensured I would have nightmares with the stories of discipline by the Nuns. She said they all come from Hell's Kitchen in New York.

"Nuns are tougher than anyone, so you better look out because they can see with eyes in the back of their heads. Four eyes, that is what they are. All you could see of flesh were the hands and part of their face."

I was terrified of learning all this and did not want to attend school. I did not know what school was like, and the nuns scared me to death when I saw them in church.

The summer of 1960 was my last time of freedom. I would no longer sit on the fence and gaze at the horses in the field. No longer would I be able to get up early and play outside to only come home for lunch and dinner. Knowing each day was getting closer to attending St. Kevin's school, I slept with one eye open every night and woke up in a cold sweat. Can a five-year-old develop anxiety?

Every day, I would sing along with Sam Cooke's "Chain Gang" song because I knew I was doomed. I'll sing the chorus: "Well, don't you know, that's the sound of the men working on the chain, ga-ang. That's the sound of the men working on the chain, ga-ang."

I felt like I was heading to prison, and the nuns were the guards. I was worried. This would be the first time alone away from the neighborhood without the freedom to come home whenever I wanted.

So, I started taking morning walks alone to my favorite places: down by the pond where we swam, where I would climb trees and catch frogs, and to the baseball field to pick grapes along the first baseline —not to eat, just to pick them off the vines.

I wanted to remember what I did daily and where I would venture to. I'd walk out to the field by the horse track and up to the farm by Sandy Lane. I knew these days would be lost forever, but I needed to experience it all again and again. The great unknown future was coming. Not having a clue what was eating at me, I felt small, facing a new world.

I trusted people all around me. I was taught to respect my elders, so older kids were my "elders." It was always "Yes, Ma'am" and "Yes, Sir." This was preached hard to me, just like "don't hit girls" by my dad. He said girls are not as big or strong as boys, and it's not fair or right to hit them. He would always look down at me with a concerned expression and ask, "Would you hit your mother?" That was enough to make me think twice.

I asked him if my sisters counted in this explanation because they sometimes got on my nerves. He said, "Especially your sisters, it's your job to protect them."

I looked up and asked if I could get an increase in my allowance for the extra work looking after my sisters. He replied, "Damn Kids!"

I had to believe in elders. That is how it always started with misplaced trust. I truly believed that someone older than me was wiser, and it was in my best interest to do exactly what I was instructed to do. I took this belief literally while walking down the Yellow Brick Road.

I was really depressed, even though there would be several of us going into the first grade. I knew where I stood compared to the other boys. I often won "King of the Hill" and fought my own fights with most of them, holding my own.. But I also knew that this school thing would put me behind everyone else. I knew I was over my head and feared being laughed at.

The other kids had already gone to Nursery school and Kindergarten, so they had experience of what school was like and knew more than I did about basic things. Meanwhile, I spent my time playing outside and exploring the neighborhood, watching horses run, or walking the track. I had a good sense of my surroundings. In the summer, I'd fish; in winter, I'd play in the snow — always alone while all the other kids went to school.

My fun days and the life I knew was about to be gone forever. Why did things have to change? I was happy just the way things had been. But now, my life was about to change, and I had no idea what changes lay ahead for me.

Chapter 5

From Barbershops To First-Day Jitters

1961

School was starting next week, so I had to get a haircut. On Saturday, when we were at grandpa's house, mom took me to the barbershop. Inside, they were two barber chairs, and on the back wall sat about eight old Italian men who were there every Saturday. I would watch them light their cigarettes with a match by striking the bottom of their shoes. People would visit the shop, and they always spoke in Italian.

My two uncles, Luigi and Alphonso, owned the shop. Luigi was 23 years older than my mom. I really liked going there as I was treated like an adult. This special treatment started when, during my first haircut, I didn't cry like the kid next to me in the other chair. There was no way I was going to embarrass my Uncle Luigi.

Uncle Luigi asked, "David, why don't you cry like that other kid?"

I replied, "Because you're my uncle Luigi!"

The place erupted with laughter.

Uncle Luigi would hand out packs of Dentyne Gum to the kids after the haircut. He was a big man with thick black hair and a huge smile.

Uncle Luigi looked like a doctor with his white smock. Uncle Alphonso would always look over, call my name, and smile while he cut someone else's hair. He was a smaller version of Luigi, and they had a round face like grandma.

Grandpa had white hair, but when he was younger, it was red on top of a long, narrow, light-skinned face. Grandma had black hair and a round face with dark skin. So, out of eleven kids, you could easily see who took after whom. Mom took after grandpa, and I took after mom. Mary took after Grandma, and Joanne after dad, poor thing.

It always took Luigi and Alphonso a while to cut someone's hair as the phone would be ringing off the hook. Whoever answered the phone would announce who was on the phone in Italian, and all the old guys would nod or laugh at the conversation they would relay. The barbershop was always bustling —busy, noisy, and so much fun to listen to all the chatter around me.

I enjoyed going places with my uncles; it was a nice change from hanging out in the kitchen. I would go every week with them. Then, go back to sit with grandpa. Uncles Richie and Thomas would pick me up and we would go driving all over town. Saturdays were nothing short of an adventure. I always slept soundly during the 25-minute drive on the way home to Warwick.

Nuns With Nightsticks

I remember as kids in the summer we always got car sick driving into Providence. We did not have air conditioning in the 1952 Chevy, so we would have the windows rolled down. The fumes from the city buses would make us sick. Joanne always threw up at least once on the drive.

I used to like holding onto the rope behind the bench seat and acting like we were being thrown around in the car. Every time dad took a turn, we acted like we were going off a cliff. He would look in the rear-view mirror to tell us to settle down.

Mom and dad always pointed out where they worked and a few buildings of interest, explaining why they were important. You could tell that they were proud to be from Providence.

The night before my first day of school was spent getting organized. Clothes were already lying on the back of my chair in my room, a light green shirt with a green tie and black pants. I packed pencils, a pad of paper and an eraser although we weren't allowed to use them.

My older sister walked with me to ensure I knew where to stand in line before entering the school. That made me feel better, knowing she would be looking after me.

We stood outside as a group and said the Pledge of Allegiance. The nuns stood in front of each line by grade, and we stood in attention position, ready to walk the death march into class. I was anxious, having zero experience in school.

I looked around at the other lines of grades; I saw kids cheerful and joyful on their first day back. I figured maybe school would not be so bad after all. All these kids got through their first day at school, so why not me?

On the first day, we learned the rules of conduct and the names of the nuns we'd have direct contact with. It sounded like an easy day the way they described how things would be. How far from the truth that was!

In our class, the boys sat on one side of the room and the girls on the other side. This made perfect sense to me because girls have cooties.

Sister Ann then instructed the boys to come to the front of the room and to line up by our birthday date. Did she say birthday? I developed a pain in my stomach and began to sweat from my forehead. I was in panic mode. I know my birthday was on Easter, so this should not be hard. I thought Easter was on the same day every year. I just needed to know the exact date in April.

I got in line with some kids born in April; I knew it was April. It just had to be.

I whispered to the kid beside me, "Hey, what day is Easter?"

He replied all-knowingly, "What year are you talking about?"

"What? What year? You mean it is different every year?" I was confused. He gave me a smirking look like I was a dummy or something. I really wanted to smack that look off his face. I thought this kid was smart.

I got in line, not in the correct order, but close enough that Sister Ann did not figure it out. I just guessed, and luckily, she did not have that information in front of her to correct me. That was a close call. As my dad would say, "Jesus, Mary and Joseph!"

Then she had the girls line up and everyone knew girls are smarter, as I found out later that week. They were up and down quicker than the boys. I thought, "What a bunch of show-offs." No wonder girls have cooties. Their big brains cause them to have cooties.

Suddenly, Sister Ann began calling each student up to her desk to ask for our phone number and the street address where we lived. I knew the house was brown and could find my way home without knowing the street address. After seven or eight boys, she called me up to her desk. Nervously, standing in front of her, she asked me for my phone number and street address. I stammered and got embarrassed. My head felt hot and I looked like a cherry tomato ready to pop. My hands were clammy, and I could not stop fidgeting, which drove Nuns nuts!

When I told her I didn't know my street address or phone number, she stared at me with a puzzled look. Not quite the smirk that kid gave me, more of a pathetic look. Kind of like I'm going to have a difficult time with this boy. It was as if she thought, "How could a 6-year-old not know their own street address and telephone number?"

I knew perfectly well that was exactly what she was thinking. Didn't she realize I did not want to be here? Hello?

Quietly, Sister Ann looked down and began writing my first letter to my parents. Are you kidding me? I have only been here for a short while, and now I am taking a note back to my parents! Damn it, I should have gone to kindergarten. I was the dumbest kid in class! And I still did not know how to whistle! I did not like all those rules and regulations.

Sister looked up at me and handed me an envelope with her name on the outside. She instructed me not to open it and read it. I thought, "No problem there, I can't read anyway."

"Your parents will reply to this note, and you will bring it back tomorrow with both of theirs' signatures." She said.

I was tempted to ask what a signature was, but no way was I going down that road.

The instructions for the code of conduct were simple.

1. Do not turn around in class; keep your eyes on the blackboard.

2. Do not use an eraser during a quiz or test. I thought, what is a quiz and a test?

3. You will address the sisters by raising your hand for permission to speak. Thinking to myself is it the left hand or the right hand?

4. You will not crumple paper; it makes too much noise. I'll rip it up that's what I'll do.

5. You will not talk to each other; you must get permission to speak.

6. You will not look up at the clock on the wall over there, pointing with her long, bony finger. I can't tell the time anyway. I go by stomach time much more reliable.

7. You must wear the uniform and keep yourselves clean and presentable. No problem, we took a bath on Saturday night, and then, as a family, we watched the TV show Bonanza. I got this covered.

8. You are to sit perfectly still and sit straight up in your chair. This is going to be a tough one.

There were many more rules; let me just say they went in from one ear and out the other. There were too many rules to remember. This school thing was stupid. The first week was rough, and the second week was nothing short of hell! I did not know how to count past ten as I only had ten fingers. I did have a cousin who had webbed fingers. The first time I met him, I thought he was half-Italian, half-lizard or something. I wondered if he could swim faster than me.

I remember going to the grocery store with my mom, and after she paid the cashier would hand her back money! I thought, "Dang, they give you money! I did not understand the concept of making change; I just saw the loot in her hand.

My mom would collect S&H Green Stamps. One time, she picked out a new toaster from the catalog proudly showing my dad her free toaster.

My dad looked at it and said, "Whoop-de-do. What? Do you like the burnt toast that mom scrapes off with a knife?"

We brought our lunch in lunch boxes, no school lunch for us. It would be peanut butter and jelly, bologna and mayo, cheese sandwiches with Velveeta and mayo, or spam sandwiches with mayo. Mayo was the main condiment in our house. Ketchup was only for hotdogs and hamburgers. We used malt vinegar on our fish and chips or fries. We purchased the milk at school. I hated carrying a lunch box and, in time, just brought a brown paper bag. You would eat fast to have more time for recess.

I missed being home, riding my bike, and going on walking adventures. Here was when I excelled in imagination. I was on a mission to find something that no one had ever seen before, to walk the land where no human had ever set foot. I pretended I was an explorer like Davy Crockett. I already had the coat and coon skin hat! Strap on my two-cap gun pistols, and away I go. What a stud I was.

Before plastic trash bags were used for residential use, there were brown paper bags from the A&P. You would wrap up coffee grounds and food scraps with the newspaper and then just put them in the paper bag. It was simple and efficient. Just like having milk delivered each morning into the milk box outside on the back steps. Such a service you do not see anymore.

How about the old Mobile gas stations? When you pulled in, three men would run out to service your car. One would pump the gas, one to check the oil, water, and tire pressure, and the other would wash the windows all around. I used to love watching them with the speed they performed their jobs.

All around me, life made sense. I could understand most things and why. But in school, they were so strict on behavior and being formal in class. There was no room for expressing yourself. It was about talking when spoken to or being called on.

The nuns followed the plan, and the structure was strict obedience. I did not understand this at the time. Life around me made some sense, but not in school. You could not question anything. You would sit up straight and face the front with eyes wide open and mouth closed. I am a mouth breather, so keeping my mouth shut was challenging, to say the least.

It seems like 99.9 % of the other kids went to kindergarten learning how to count to thirty, add and subtract small numbers, able to identify letters and the sounds they make to form words.

I did not know the letters in the alphabet. Learning how to tell time was difficult for me. I had no idea how to tell the time. I just figured it was breakfast, lunch, or dinner time when my stomach was hungry.

The alphabet was the first song I had to memorize. I still sing the Alphabet song to myself when I need to file something. May the Lord help me if I have to say the Alphabet backwards in a traffic stop. But I hear that is a myth. But I'm not going to find out if it happens to be true somewhere out there.

Printing letters was not an easy task for me. All my letters had a weird slant to them. The letters confused me, and I had trouble with the letters m, n, and w. I was happy to see the alphabet secure at the top over the blackboard as it was my first cheat sheet. Printing was very difficult as I could not make them look like the ones over the blackboard.

At first, I was holding the pencil incorrectly and Sister corrected this. But I could not stop the letters from having the wrong shape with a slant. I thought I would never be able to print my name, ever! But Sister's persistence paid off for me. But that whole story is coming up!

Then reading came and I did not know how to read. I ended up in the special reading class with three other kids who did not attend kindergarten. I was embarrassed and ashamed that I was not up to speed like the other kids.

A special reading class meant to me that I was slow and stupid. The things I knew about in life had no bearing in school. I felt like I was way over my head, and this caused me to be nervous and self-conscious.

For the reading and training, they used a Jack and Jill book that was 3 feet high, and we would sit on the floor and take turns reading from it. I did not care for Jill because all girls have cooties.

We went to Mass every day before the start of class. For some reason, my intestines would make a growling noise during mass every day, and it was loud enough to hear in two pews. I handled this properly by turning around and saying, "Who was that?" No one figured I was the one with the musical stomach. Could it have been the Cocoa Puffs?

Mass was confusing as to when we were supposed to use the Kneeler, stand, and sit. I just followed everyone else on what to do. Everything was so confusing that I could not read that well.

In time, I learned the mass routine. Of course, I did not understand everything due to the Tridentine Mass. This was also known as the Traditional Latin Mass, the Roman Rite Mass of the Catholic Church. This mass was in the Roman Missal until 1962.

I learned how to mumble in unison with everyone else. Thank you, Vatican 2, for changing the mass to English. When I heard the mass in English, I thought, "This is all they have been saying?"

It seemed so magical in Latin. Now, I had to mumble in English instead of Latin just when I learned how to speak Latin, well sort of.

Chapter 6

Family Differences and Lasting Impacts

Adults never called me by my first name. My hair was red, and both my parents had red hair. Some adults used to call me Red—easier than knowing my first name. The Ice cream man was Scottie, and when I would come up to the truck, he would smile and say, "Okay Red, what will it be today?"

In good weather, we would play outside after dinner, and then Scottie would roll down the street and get mobbed by a bunch of kids. We would eat our ice cream and talk in small groups. After we were done the mothers would yell out for the kids to come home for the night.

Once a man approached my mom and me at the A&P grocery store. He said, "Wow you sure have red hair, kid. Where do you get your red hair from?" I did not know for sure.

I said, "From the sun." Wondering why this man is asking me about my hair. I did not know about genetics back then, but the sun made perfect sense to me. My mom and the man laughed, but I did not know why.

I made my mom a little mad in the store that same day. I asked her why all the old Italian women were sitting in chairs by the front door, pointing directly at the group of women. Of course, I talked loudly. "Mom, do you know they all have mustaches?" I assumed it must be an Italian thing. She told me to stop staring at people as it was impolite. "But they have mustaches Mom!"

Over the next few weeks, I had enough of Jack and Jill and went to stay with the other kids in class. Okay maybe it was longer. Then, one day, an announcement came over the speaker in the room. I thought it was God talking as I looked straight up at the ceiling, not where the speaker was. So that thing hanging on the wall is a speaker? Imagine that! May wonders never cease.

We had to attend the church for a special assembly, and it was just for the first and second grades. Apparently, there were a lot of kids who were getting injured watching the greatest show on TV, The Three Stooges. We sat there as Sister Margret, the Mother Superior, spoke to us. She said, "Raise your hand if you watch the Three Stooges." Every kid raised up a hand, some both hands, and she murmured on the microphone, "Oh My!" She continued, "Children across this nation are poking other children in the eyes and losing their eyesight! Did you know that? This is serious, and you should not poke anyone in the eyes." I was still focused on what a nation was. Why did she not just say Rhode Island? As far as I was concerned, this was the world!

Suddenly, a kid named Tommy raised his hand in the front pew. He yelled, "Mother Superior, when someone goes to poke you in the eyes, you just hold up your hand like this and block it." All the kids were laughing and knew this to be true.

Just then appeared two nuns who swooped down on Tommy and pulled him out of the pew by his ears! They both had hands on him as they left the church. I thought, so that is how they do it, double team and come out of nowhere to grab you and to take you away for the punishment. It was fast and stealth-like. I remember this every time watching a Ninja movie.

On the walk home that day, I asked my older sister what kind of punishment they would give poor Tommy. She said that you usually extend your hand for a minor offense, and they will whack the front and back of your hand a few times with the ruler. They will do the same thing for a serious offense but use the pointer. Further punishment would be to bang your head against the cement block wall a few times. If that does not work, then they will call your parents. There you have it, some of the rules to live by. Then we stopped walking, and she looked me straight in the eyes. "But never, ever be sent to the principal's office!"

"What happens there?" I meekly asked. I was terrified of these Nuns already.

"You do not want to know. Just do not go to the principal's office if you know what is good for you." She sounded like a grown-up, so it was in one ear and out the other. Okay, first joke you learn in Catholic school.

What is black and white, black and white, and black and white? A nun rolling down the hill. Come on now, it is a first-grade joke.

Remember when I said my parents had a mixed marriage? Well, during this time period, Italians and Irish did not get along very well. The Irish looked down on Italians. Now, I was going to a Catholic School that was Irish by name and most of the kids were Irish. The kids at school knew I was half Italian, obviously with the hand talk thing.

One day after school, I came home to find my mom washing dishes with a sink full of soap suds. I said to mom, "I have a question?" She looked down for a second and said, "Go ahead and ask." I looked at her and asked, "Mom, what is a WOP?" In half a second, this huge hand comes out of nowhere, wet and soapy, and she slaps me right across the face. I was stunned by the speed of her soapy hand.

"Ma! What did you do that for?" I said, teary-eyed.

"That is a bad word for an Italian. Never say that word to me again!"

"Okay I won't say it again." Thinking, what the heck was that all about? I stood there for a few seconds to compose myself and to ask another question. "But I have another question to ask you?"

"What is it now?" Mom sternly looked down at me. She was not a happy camper. "Mom, what is a DAGO?"

Smack across the face again. What is going on here, I thought. It is just a question! "Ma! What did you hit me for?" This is just not my day.

"It is a bad word for an Italian do not repeat it in this house or ever. Where did you hear these words?"

With tears in my eyes, I said, "They called me that at school today. I just want to know what it means, that's all. Why are they calling me these words? What have I done?" Mom looked down at me and said what all mothers back then said to their children. "Sticks and stones will break your bones, but words will never hurt you." I wanted to say that it is not true your hand hurt a lot. But there was no way I was going down that road. I thought note to myself, never ask questions from mom when she is washing dishes.

About a week later, I heard the song Banana Boat performed by Harry Belafonte. I was very upset about this song. It went, "Dago, dago Daylight come, and we want to go home. Day is a day, is a day, is a day is a dago." Years, and I mean years later, I finally looked at the lyrics. Oh! Was I surprised by that! It was day-o not dago.

Usually, I would ride my bike with Mick when we got home from school. We would venture out and cross Sandy Lane and try and get lost then find our way back home. One time, we found a lot of furniture and loose papers in the woods—a lot of trash strewn all over both sides of the road. I looked at Mick and picked up some papers, but we could not read cursive writing. I said, "I bet it is in German, and they bombed this place." He figured I was right, and we could not wait to tell the other kids about the German Bombing.

On one of our adventures Mick and I were walking in a field and found a huge whelk shell. These are slow-moving sea snails that open and devour quahogs. We put it to our ears to hear the ocean. We could not figure out how this shell ended up in a field. We didn't realize we were only 50 feet from Oakland Beach. From West Shore Road, it was 2 miles to Saltwater Beach. Every day was an adventure; our imaginations would get ahead of us. Everything we came upon was new and exciting. We were explorers on a mission.

We used to collect baseball cards and trade them. It was not really trading as we used to toss them one at a time against a wall, and if your card covered up the other card, then you would keep both cards. The other way was to flip them, and the winner would be the one with the picture on the front if the other card ended up on the stat side. Pitching pennies against a wall was great fun; the closest to the wall would keep the other person's penny. You would get several guys to play at the same time and make more money. When I got older, nickels, dimes, and quarters were used. It was a lot easier than shooting craps like some kids did in high school, but that involved using paper money, which meant a lot more to lose.

Dad was very frugal and demanded that we use toilet paper as little as possible. Even showed us how to fold it over and how much to use. We had a cesspool, and dad blamed me for clogging it up because I used too much toilet paper. They would not let me go in the backyard to see them pump it out. But I did get a chance across the street when they had to empty their cesspool. It was a huge hole, and it went as far as China! Joanne was with me as I looked straight down the hole. Joanne wanted to see down there as well, and I told her she needed to move closer to see what was down there. I kept telling her to move closer. She inched her way closer and closer.

Then it happened and she fell right into the cesspool. My first thought was a new word I had learned. Shit! Am I going to get it this time? I ran home to tell dad that Joanne had fallen in, and she was crying. She was so scared. I hid when the firefighters came and did not want them to know I was involved. I did not need to see those guys again, no way. I got the leather belt on my bare back for this stunt. Joanne had to take an extra bath that week. Okay I thought it was funny, and maybe I coerced her to get closer and fall in. To this day, she swears I pushed her in, and that is why I got the belt. I must have blocked that from my memory when I ran home.

We went to church every Sunday, and Joanne was nothing short of trouble being a four-year-old. It was difficult for her to remain still and quiet. One Sunday, a lady sitting in the pew in front of us was wearing a big hat, and Joanne could not stop touching it. She tugged on it a couple of times and the lady would turn around. Dad was furious and motioned for me to grab her hand and stop her. Then Joanne started singing Happy Birthday over and over.

Dad's face was red, and mom was horrified. She got a spanking before she entered the car with no understanding of why she was getting whacked. Like other siblings Mary and I laughed as she was getting hit. Not too loud so Dad would not have a reason to involve us. Whenever one of us got whacked, the other two would snicker. It was just our way.

Joanne was very sociable at this time. We were eating in a restaurant, and a tall man came walking in. Joanne goes up to the man, stopping him in his tracks. She looked up at him and asked a question.

"Hi Mister, are you married?" The restaurant erupted in laughter, and Joanne decided to sing a song right there in front of everyone. Joanne looked like Shirley Temple and got away with it. She could pull it off. She got a round of applause from everyone in the restaurant. She then sat down at the table smiling while my dad, with his red face and mom's open mouth, just sat frozen.

Every year both sides of the family would have a family reunion. Now, the Irish side had the reunion at a park. I was very upset with mom as she purchased white slacks and a button-down shirt for me to wear. We are going to a park, why would I wear this? She spoke warmly and said, "It is your father's family, and we must make a good impression." We were instructed to bring and eat our own food. Very strange not to share food with other family members. I never had to dress up like this for mom's side of the family. When we walked up to the family, we could see them sharing food with each other. Why did they tell us to bring our own food to eat? They would not eat food prepared by an Italian. I was feeling like a stranger within my dad's family. They were my family, right? We were also at the furthest table away from everyone else.

My dad's family was not happy that he married an Italian. My little sister and I went to play with our cousins. We did not know them very well as we would only see most of them once a year. This was due to the fact of how my mom was being treated by my dad's family. To explain this, I guess it would be standoffish. You know, somewhat reserved, cold, and unfriendly around my mom. Like they did not know how to talk to her. Which in turn came out to no way they wanted food prepared by mom. We all felt the tension like walking into an invisible wall.

Joanne and I walked up to about six cousins around our age to hang out. They moved away from us when we got closer. We walked towards them again, and they moved away from us. Then, on the third time, I got the hint, so we left and hung out with mom. We are supposed to be family, so what is up with this? I never ever felt a part of my dad's family and dad did not talk much about them. He became an outsider as well with his own family. A real shame as my dad came from a family with ten other siblings, just like mom, and now, he was alone. I never realized this until right now writing this down. It explains how my dad felt about his family. He was an outcast due to marrying an Italian.

Joanne and I started running around, and I slipped on some grass a few times. Mom was horrified to see me when we returned to our table. "David! You have grass stains all over your pants, and your shoes are muddy. Look at your shirt!" I thought, OK, it is time to let mom know this was all wrong having me wear this outfit. "Mom, I am a kid in a park and wearing a button-down shirt, white pants, and hard slippery shoes. What do you expect?" I had her, and she knew it; she just had me sit next to her and hugged me. "You were right, David." I did not hear that very often. I was right?

Going home, we all sat silent looking out the windows and no clowning around. We did not feel right and knew we were being treated differently. I was happy to go right to bed and get out of those fancy grass-stained pants.

Chapter 7
A Dangerous Play

When my parents got married, they went to rent an apartment in Providence. But they were denied by Italian and Irish landlords. Mix marriage, no real surprise there. No one would rent to them. Finally, a Jewish Landlord let them rent an apartment. Due to this, dad instilled in us kids a high regard and respect for the Jewish people. This was pure proof of the hatred that Italians and Irish had for each other.

Back around the 1880s, the reasons for the hatred between Irish and Italians were two main reasons: economy and religious faith. First, the Irish migration of the 1840s put them on good footing in their communities by the time the Italian migration came in the 1880s. With jobs and local politics, the Irish communities had power with a firm foundation. The Italians had to work for less and work longer hours than the Irish. Most worked low end labor jobs as the Irish had the pick of the litter. As the years went into the 1900s, they both would fight for jobs and local power on somewhat equal footing. The Italians were becoming Americans and speaking English. When you do not speak the language, it is difficult to advance in the types of lucrative positions that would be available. It takes a while for kids that came over to learn English. Many of the parents still spoke broken English at best. The second reason some of the Irish were Protestant and they despised the Pope in Italy.

Back when my parents had the apartment, the local priest of the Parish wanted to meet them and welcome them to the community. When the priest knocked on the door, Mary, who was around four years old, opened the door. She asked why he was there and found out he wanted to talk to dad. She said to the Priest, "Come in and I will take you to him." Mary went right to the bathroom door with the priest behind her. She opened the door and introduced the priest to my father who was sitting on the toilet! It was a very embarrassing moment for dad. He exclaimed, "Wa – What are you doing Mary?"

"Shut the door right now!" shouted Dad. The priest turned red, feeling ashamed of the entire situation.

I can hear the song by Rodgers & Hammerstein, "Getting to know you. Getting to know all about you." Looking at dad, I said, "What in the world are you eating for breakfast?" I was minding my own business eating cocoa puffs when my mom served my dad kidneys on toast. One of his favorite English meals he would have for breakfast.

"Dad, the smell is ruining the taste of my cocoa puffs!"

He just said, "MMMMM good! Do you want some as well?"

Nuns With Nightsticks

One thing is for sure. My older sister and I would go out and pick blueberries for breakfast. At this time, Mom served us shredded wheat. This was before they had bite-sized shredded wheat. We would put sugar on first then the blueberries on top of the shredded wheat, but they would fall off when we added the milk. We did not know we were supposed to squeeze the bag to make it shredded. Years later, I saw someone squeeze the shredded wheat bag and I screamed, "What are you doing?" I learned how to eat shredded wheat from that day on. Perhaps I inherited the literal thing from mom.

I did not care for steak at all when I was a kid. The steak just seemed to taste funny. It turns out that Mom said it was steak, but no, it was liver and onions NOT steak! I was in my twenties before I had the courage to order steak in a restaurant.

Some of the popular toys in 1961 were the Betsy Wetsy doll and the slip-and-slide. Of course, we did not get either one of these. I received a cool brown dump truck and was happy to get it. I got a yo-yo and carried it in my pocket for any chance to practice. It was the first of many. We hung out and showed each other what we could do with them. I learned how to walk the dog with my yo-yo and sometimes did the around-the-world trick.

The Italian family reunions were a lot of fun. Counting my grandparents, uncles, and cousins born by 1961, there were about 82 people in attendance. We would go to a large park, and all the cars would have their trunks open. All the tables would be full of food, and we would share and eat until our belts were too tight. We would have several tables full of food like salads, side dishes, pasta, and pizza served at room temperature with just sauce on dough, which tasted great. Also, deli meats, grilled meats, and loaves of Italian bread were also on the menu. Then the one best table in the world would be the Italian pastries. Zeppole is a fried dough ball topped with powdered sugar. Sfogliatelle is a shell-shaped flaky crust pastry filled with orange flavored ricotta, Baci di Dama are hazelnut cookies, and Migliaccio ricotta cake. The uncles would play Bocce ball and drink beer and wine to work off the food. To start the game, you would throw out the Bocchino, or as some call it, the Pallino (little ball). It was an honor for me to throw out the Bocchino. I was now a man! Okay maybe not, but that is how I felt that first time anyway.

Some of the uncles would play Scopa with a deck of Neapolitan cards. Scopa in Italian means to sweep. In small communes in Italy, you can still see people gathered around a table exchanging swear words and bantering over a heated game of Scopa. You would play with 2 to 4 players or two teams. You would listen for the person who takes the last card as they would say, "Fatto Scopa!" and get an extra point. Fatto means done in Italian. My uncle Thomas would sit at the table next to the cooler filled with Narragansett beer. He would wear a skimmer boater straw hat with a white tank undershirt complete with Bermuda shorts, black socks, and sandals. He would sit there, mumble, and swear in Italian while he played Scopa! Even as a young child, I knew he was making fashion faux pas. They would have my dad get drinks for them. I can hear it now, "Hey brother-in-law, get me a glass of wine." My dad would jump up and get it for them. Italians were not fond of the Irish, so he was always called to duty. It never got out of hand because they did not want to hurt their little sister. Mom was loved by all who knew her.

We hit the pastry table after eating and playing bocce ball and scopa. Then, a couple of my uncles would pull out the guitars and play music with all of us singing until it got dark. I would look around at everyone singing and think what a cool family.

The first trip to the principal's office occurred a few weeks into first grade. It was not, I repeat not my fault. Not my problem; Sister Ann had it out for me.

"Mr. O'Rielly, you are doing it wrong. How many times must I tell you?" screamed Sister Ann. I was mad, and she really got under my skin. She is always watching me. I said, "No, you are doing it all wrong, and it doesn't make any sense to me." I had learned how to count on my fingers from 1 through 5, starting with the thumb, not the index finger. It was how they count in Italy, but I did not know this at the time. Sister then whispered to calm me down. "Who taught you this, your father?"

"No Sister Ann, I learned from my uncles!" in a proud and loud voice. "I am the teacher, and what I say is the gospel in this class." in her screeching voice. "You will do what I tell you to do. You count with your index finger first, NOT your thumb." She was pointing her bony finger right in my face. Now she is bringing the Bible in on this. The rest of the class suddenly became mouth breathers. My rep went up a few rungs. Not fair, I thought. Now, I was excited, and my hands were waving all over the place, gesturing to make my points perfectly clear. She had enough of me at this point.

"Stop waving your hands around when you are speaking! You sound and look like a stupid Italian." Did I just hear what I think she said? What? Did she just call my family stupid? I know I am, but certainly not my family. In a fierce, squeaky voice that only a six-year-old could have, I said, "I always talk with my hands and my uncles are not stupid! I count the thumb first!"

She then grabbed me by the collar and instructed me in a very polite manner with her piercing Eyes. "You're going to the principal's office right now." I took a deep breath and walked along with her like I had a choice in the matter. I was so mad, and Mary told me not to go to the principal's office. Now I am struggling to get free, and sister has a vice grip on me. Oh, if I were only taller. I was terrified of what would happen next. I was in a rage to defend my family at any cost. Mother Superior was at her desk when we walked in. She was tall and sat perfectly straight. She had a stoic look, and I was forced to stand right in front of her. She asked sister why I was standing in front of her. I thought, why don't you just ask me? Sister Ann explained my indiscretions. I was outnumbered and figured I'd better just take it. And take it I did. Just a few whacks of the ruler on my hands front and back. Dad prepared me well for this useless exercise in punishment. I thought, is this all they got? I can do this all day long. Now, bringing home a second note may not have been a big thing at your home, but Mary was a practicing Saint. She never got into trouble at school, was popular, and got along with everyone. I, on the other hand, was Satan's Seed twice removed. All I remember is what my dad said loudly, "This is why I wanted only the Nuns to teach our children!" That is when I repeated the words I recently heard from my father, "Well Whoop-DE-Do!" Smack, bang, to your room Satan! I went to my room, thinking I needed to wear corduroy pants all the time for the extra padding that they provided. I ended up getting in trouble a few days later. During recess, I liked to play with my pocketknife and a few of us would play a form of mumblety-peg. We would face each other about 5 feet away and throw the pocketknife to stick in the ground and the other player had to put one of their feet where the knife had landed without moving their other foot. Then, on the other person's turn, the knife had to be thrown towards the other player. The player lost if the knife did not stand up or if the opponent would be unable to stand where the knife was tossed. We tossed the knife to get it as close to the other player as possible. Obviously, the Nuns considered this dangerous. I objected when the nun, at the time, pulled me by my collar and took my knife away from me. Then I got my hands smacked front and back with the ruler. She did not give it back either, but I had plenty of pocket-knives.

Chapter 8
The Difficult Times

On January 20th, 1961, John F Kennedy was inaugurated as President of the United States, and for the first time, I felt proud to be Irish and Catholic. However, not on the way walking to school. Protestant schoolkids in buses would come streaming down the street and see us Catholic kids walk and yell out the windows, "Hey, you dirty little Catholics!" Some would have their heads sticking out the window with tongues sticking out. In a quick response, I used the Italian arm salute called L'Ombrello, not the middle finger. You bend your arm in an L shape with the fist high in the air. Then, with your other hand, you slap the bicep. I am also Italian, you jerks. My other favorite hand gesture was taking the back of your right hand, holding it under your chin, and quickly flinging it towards the person you are disgusted with. It is called a chin flick or 'Non mi interessa' in Italian. Basically, stating I am done with you! Or I don't care! I Just remembered; I had a waiter do that to me in Capri. He did it as a joke because he was flirting with my wife. I gave him a look that I knew this gesture. He flung the hand to the side of his chin, not towards me. I ended up getting a free bottle of wine out of it, so all was good. Well, two bottles would have been better.

David Michael O'Rielly

Rhode Island and John Fitzgerald Kennedy shared many experiences over the years. In Newport, he married Jacqueline Bouvier on September 12th, 1953, at St. Mary's church in Newport with 750 guests. The wedding was presided over by Archbishop Richard Cushing. The summer White House years were spent at Hammersmith Farm in Newport. This was a 28-room Victorian mansion built in 1887 by John Auchincloss, the great-grandfather of Jackie's stepfather, Hugh D. Auchincloss. This is where Jacqueline spent her time as a child. The farm was located at 225 Harrison Avenue, where they held the wedding reception. They would arrive in the Marine Corps helicopter when they would visit the farm. In 1976, Jacqueline's mother, Janet Lee Auchincloss, sold the main house (mansion) and moved into one of the guest houses on the farm called "The Castle."

Camelot rang true during the time of the Kennedy's in government. The power of hope for our future was bright. We were entering a new age of awareness and technology. The idea that real vision can survive during our times of fear and doubt, with the Atom bomb at the ready, was profound. Communism was getting strong, but Camelot ruled the day. In April 1961, 1400 Cuban exiles launched a failed invasion of Cuba. The adults were all talking about this and the Russian influence they had on Cuba. President Kennedy did not inform the international community of the invasion, so he withheld the air support needed to win. I did not know what questions to ask or why I should be scared. I just looked into my parents' faces, and that told me all I needed to know. This was serious and I needed to behave now more than ever. Tensions were very high, and I did not need to tick off dad.

We prayed more in school for our President and Country, and saying the Pledge of Allegiance under the flag meant more than it did before. The Nuns seemed to stand a lot taller to protect their kids. In time, the adults moved on to other pressing matters of daily life. I guess we were all amazed when President Kennedy announced the Apollo program to put a man on the moon before the end of the 1960s. This was unbelievable that we could do this. Everyone felt proud to be an American with this goal in mind. This gave us hope where before we were afraid and worried about our future. I was surprised to find out the moon was not made of cheese. I never cared for Swiss cheese because of this. The moon freaked me out. One time, we were driving home from the beach, and I looked out the window and saw the full, bright moon. When we turned a corner, it was still there.

The further we went the moon was still there. I was terrified as I thought the moon was following us and wondered what would happen when the moon caught up to us. My dad's go-to drink was called a Presbyterian. I assumed Presbyterians were whisky makers and that all Protestants like to drink whisky, just like all Italians like Chianti. Irish and Italian in one household made it very confusing for me.

David Michael O'Rielly

It was weird when my dad would talk with a cockney accent and tell humorous stories. The first time he did this, my little sister and I were at the kitchen table waiting for dinner. He started speaking in a cockney accent. This scared the both of us. I looked at him with a quizzical look and said, "Dad, is that you? Where are you, Dad?" Dad had totally transformed himself in his face and mannerisms. I did not recognize him. I knew he was my dad, but where was he?

He told a lot of funny stories over the years, always in Cockney. It did make watching English movies a lot easier to understand. He was proud to be English like Nanna. One of the biggest news of the day was Roger Maris of the New York Yankees hit his 61st home run against my team the Boston Red Sox! I was happy that he broke Babe Ruth's record but upset it had to happen in the last game of the season. Baseball was over, so I put a baseball in my oiled glove and tied it up tight until the next season. This way the glove would fit perfectly with the right size pocket to catch a ball. I liked playing basketball but could not dribble without walking, so I would draw a walking violation. The only dribbling I could do was dribbling slowly down my chin.

When we went to Grandpa's house, I was old enough to walk down the street to the local grocery store. There we would get ice cream or candy. Next door to this was a bar, and they had a boccie ball court in the back of the bar adjacent to the street. A high fence sheltered the court from the street so onlookers could not easily see the game. On top of the fence, they had a bench, and men would sit up on top, yelling and screaming. Talk about a lively neighborhood. It was always safe to walk in Italian areas of Providence.

We got into trouble one Saturday for ringing doorbells. Well, it was just one house that we did this. It was the Witch's house. We would run up the stoop from the sidewalk, ring it, and run back to grandpas. It was a Witch's house, so I did not see why I was in trouble. I was told she was an old Italian woman, and I was driving her nuts with the doorbell. The last time I heard older kids tell me about Witches, "Go ahead and do it!" was all I heard. I felt extremely guilty after this and ashamed of myself. Got sucked in again.

Back during the Depression in the 1930s, grandpa and grandma helped feed the people in the neighborhood. Grandma and grandpa showed them how to make pasta and how to grow vegetables. In the meantime, they fed many people who did not know how to grow vegetables or make pasta until they could do it themselves. This Witch was not a Witch after all but rather a dear friend of grandmas. I learned how the neighborhood banded together during the Depression. The relationships they developed had changed lives forever. I did not know about my grandparents helping the neighbors during the Depression. I found out about this from an older cousin years later. He was working at Home Depot in Connecticut. A customer came in and asked about his name tag. He said, "Did your family live on Hendrick Street in

Providence?" My cousin replied, "Yes, as a matter of fact." The customer then put out his hand to shake my cousin's hand. He told him of the stories he had heard about our family during the Depression and how they fed the families in the neighborhood. He said, "Our family talks about this every year at our family reunion about the neighborhood and your family. Our family owes your family a lot." I was proud when I heard this story. I wondered why I had never heard this story before. My cousin told the other cousins at our family reunion, as no one had ever heard this before. That made me even more proud. I learnt that if we live a simple life with respect and honor, we will live in the hearts of people forever.

Chapter 9

Playtime Memories and School Stages

1962

I did not know the kid who sat behind me in Second Grade. It was our first week back to school. I was in the front row as it was easier for Sister to hit me. I wanted to sit in the back but was in the front row because I was fighting on the playground during playtime. I did not know what was going on, but trouble always followed me. I brought my Beany and Cecil hat to school in the first week back to school. Beany and Cecil was a cartoon. Beany Boy had a hat called the Beany Copter, complete with a helmet and propeller. Beany would always get into trouble and would call out for his favorite friend, Cecil the green seasick serpent with a slight lisp.

Cecil would always reply, "I'm a commin; Beany-boy!" You would put the hat on your head, and it had two plastic blades on top of the hat. You would wind it up, and it would fly off your head. Man! It was cool. It was so cool. Another kid liked it and took it from me. He was older, but in my neighborhood, that was not okay. I had to get my beany hat back at any cost!

First fight, first week, front row. Good morning, Sister!

David Michael O'Rielly

One day, the kid behind me was fidgeting and was shaking his desk. Then, I heard him make a loud, nerve-racking sound. It scared the bejesus out of me. Some of the kids near him started to scream and cough. I had to turn around and look; I just had to. Rule number 1. do not turn around. I turned around anyway, and I could see he was wearing a beard, and I turned back. I thought that couldn't be right, so I turned around again and saw it was really vomit. I quickly looked back to the front as the other kids were freaking out. Sister had her hands full as she pulled him out of his chair and went straight to the nurse's office.

Mother Superior came in to calm us down. The janitor came in with sawdust and spread it over the desktop and floor. The smell was so bad due to the sawdust. We could barely breathe. We shut up faster than a fastball from Bill Monbouquette, or Monbo, for short, which was his nickname.

My favorite player on the Red Sox, hands down, was #8 Carl Yastrzemski in his second year with the Sox. I would be Yaz, the great left-handed left-field player when I played baseball. I was not ashamed to be a lefty since Yaz was also a lefty.

In second grade, the nuns decided that I had to change my writing hand from left to right. My printing looked like I was using my toes. All the letters went this way and that way. No matter how hard I tried, I could not duplicate what Sister Ann wrote on the chalkboard for us to copy. All you could hear in class was NO! NO! No! Mr. Orielly,

NOOOOOOOO! It reached the point that my face looked like I got sunburned every day in class. When your face and hair are red, and you have many freckles, you really stand out.

The nuns sent me home with a note on this, and my parents went to school to get the facts. Only the Devil writes left-handed. The note stated we are unable to properly teach David how to print due to being left-handed. Please call to set up a time to come to school to discuss this. Dad had to take off work, not a good thing for me. Why was I the only left-hander in my family? I was cursed. A redhead with freckles and also left-handed. And I still can't whistle!

In Rhode Island, your family is usually your best friend, and you hang out a lot with family. In other words, I had a cousin come to the house to make me right-handed—no such luck. When I threw a baseball, it was left-handed. I could not throw the ball from my right hand. I also could not catch a ball with a left-handed glove. I was Satan's seed.

After an hour or so, my cousin told my dad; sorry, he is left-handed. My mom called Sister Ann and told her that I was left-handed and unable to be right-handed. Sister was not a happy camper and told my parents she would do what she could, but my writing was horrific because she could not teach a left-hander.

Apparently, Satan was left-handed, and I was the seed of Satan. Since I had such bad penmanship, I thought about my sister writing a letter to future teachers, saying that it was her fault that I had bad penmanship. But for a kid, I did not have the stones to ask.

At St. Kevin's, we had an area to play baseball with a backstop during recess. It was a small area, so you had a pitcher and a batter, and everyone else would be on the field. You did not run the bases too small of an area. So, the batter would stay in the batters' box until they were called out. After you hit the ball in the batter's box, you would lay your bat over the plate, and when someone threw the ball back towards home plate, they would let it roll. If it hit the bat, you were out. Then, the person who hits the bat would be the next batter. Other ways to be called out were three strikes or if the ball was caught in the air. Otherwise, you would just stay in the batter's box and hit the ball. If called out on strikes, the pitcher would be the next batter, or if the ball was caught in the air, that person would bat next.

Another game we played was called War. You would get two big guys and two little guys like me who would sit on top of their shoulders. We would play war by trying to knock the other kid off the shoulders. Looking back, I can see why this was dangerous.

One time, I soon found out how sneaky the Nuns were. We got called out for playing war on the grass adjacent to the hardtop, next to recess's full glory, with kids running around playing tag and other activities. One of the sisters monitoring play came up to all four of us. She had us line up in a single line. One at a time, she stood on the tips of our toes and pushed us backward so we would fall to the ground. There was no way to defend yourself with this shrewd move. It was Nun jujitsu. You could not even see their feet when they did this. I had instant respect for them the first time this happened to me. Why did I never learn?

Mom and dad were talking about one of my aunts who was seeing a Rheumatologist. Mom said that she was in a lot of pain. So, prayers were offered until we heard what the doctor had to say. I did not think this was such a big deal. She needed help, but there were plenty of family members who could help her when she needed them. I thought the word was spelled Roomatologist and that she was seeing a Doctor of Interior Design. I thought she needed help rearranging the furniture. This way, she would not have any more aches and pains.

The hottest toy in 1962 was a Chatty Cathy Doll that would not shut up. The Etch-A-Sketch was a gift for all three of us. You see, we received one new toy for a birthday and Christmas. The rest of the toys were hand-me-downs from older cousins who were still in good condition—wrap it up, and they're new. We also received clothes from them as well and we never complained because we got to wear our older cousins' clothes and play with the same toys they did. In a way, it was an honor to do so. Good enough for them so certainly good enough for us. Our extended family was very close. We did everything together and visited on every holiday.

It was a highlight that in our family, we still have an original Shepard's Department store box that we exchange between the three of us each year at Christmas. God forbid that this box should disappear or get ruined. It is our precious memory of Rhode Island. You know, the place where Jesus grew up and was my neighbor.

My dad came home with a prototype of the Super Ball. A little smaller than a baseball and larger than the ones that came onto the market in 1964. It was army green and hard as a rock. You could not squeeze it and did not have to put air into it like a basketball. He worked at US Rubber and brought it home for me to play with. It was on a Friday, so it was a nice weekend surprise just for me!

We were in the driveway, and he was bouncing the ball, screaming, "Look how high it bounces. David, watch this." Each time, the ball would go higher and higher. I took it and bounced it all the way down the street towards the pond. Two older kids around sixteen years old took the ball from me. No one had ever seen anything like this. One of them threw it down hard, and it bounced into the pond about six feet from the shore. They laughed and said sorry kid about your ball. I went home without it. Dad said, "Where is the ball I gave you to play with?" I told him it was in the pond, and he freaked out and said, "We must go and get it right now! His face was beet red, and he was in a panic mode. "I must bring the ball back to work by Monday! I was not supposed to take it out of the lab!" He ran down there and made those two boys go into the water and retrieve the ball. My dad was sure relieved when he examined the ball and did not see any marks on it. I don't think he ever brought anything back home again.

One day, a few of us were walking around the neighborhood, and we went up to a 4-year-old kid. Next to him was a wiener dog, the dachshund. I told him that the dog was called a wiener dog. I asked him if he knew why, and he just shook his head no. The other guys backed me up. I said, pointing to the dog that this is where hot dogs come from. He looked confused, and I said the next time your family has hot dogs, it will be this here dog. The little boy ran away screaming, and we ran off before his mom could catch us. I felt bad about the joke but then remembered the fire alarm and justified it. I don't justify it now, however.

A few of the kids had homemade wooden push cars. One kid would be in the driver's seat, and another would push from behind. We would gather at the telephone pole with that dang fire alarm on it. We would go fast and ram the cars into each other. When we got tired of this, occasionally, someone would have firecrackers, and we would divide them up, then have a war and throw them at each other. Other times, we just threw small rocks at each other in the street. This does explain a lot of the scars I have on my head. I am surprised this did not knock some sense into me.

Other games we would play outside were tag, hide and seek, marbles, and King of the Hill. Another game, leapfrog, was good for a few minutes, but you would get bored doing it. Playing Cowboys, with the good guys against the bad guys, was the best of all. You would wear your cowboy hat with a pair of cap guns and run all over the neighborhood. Other times, we would play Crusaders. You would take a piece of wood from a picket fence and use the metal trash can lid as a shield; another game was Cops and Robbers, and I never lost with my Tommy gun.We would get a bunch of guys together and play two baseball teams up at the baseball field by the pond. Getting a team together was never easy due to a lack of planning.

On a rainy day, we would play with jacks and pickup sticks. We would take turns looking through a view master or a kaleidoscope. We had board games like Uncle Wiggly or play Tiddlywinks and Dominoes, as there was plenty to do with your imagination. Screw that being a literal thing I had ideas.

Any adult had the power and authority to correct your behavior back then. If they saw something out of line, they would step right in. As kids, we were taught respect and honor and were monitored most of the time without us even knowing about it. Kids were not treated as fragile little things. Play could be a rough and tumble affair. Our parents went through the same thing: a kid must remain a kid while playing and leave them alone but have a watchful eye. You knew everyone in the neighborhood and who to stay away from.

Later in the year, our class had a school song to present to the entire school. I was not too happy about getting in front of people on stage. Not my cup of tea. But worse than that, we had to go behind the curtain and sit in front of a mirror to put on lipstick. All of us boys were in an uproar over this. Lipstick like my mom puts on? Sister Clara, our second-grade teacher, stood tall and said, "The audience will be unable to see your lips without the lipstick, so put it on well. All stage actors do this."

I had just one thing to do during this song, just one thing! The song was about a dog. My part was to leave off stage and grab a huge stuffed dog half my size, then hold it up for the audience on the last verse of the song.

Sister Clara was standing below the stage providing directions. First, she set the tone of our song with a pitch pipe. While singing, we had to put our hands up next to our ears and move them back and forth to act like we had dog ears. The time for me to grab the dog and hold it up was soon approaching. I forgot all about it as I was blinded by the lights. I was frozen, standing in front of the whole school. There were so many people staring at me that I froze and forgot everything. Talk about deer frozen still by blinding headlights. Same thing for me! I just stood there with Sister Clara, yelling, "Get the dog, go and get the dog!"

She was pointing at me, and I looked at her, yelling back, "Dog? What dog?" She then lost it and said, "The song is about a dog, and it's off-stage." At this point, everyone is looking and hearing us during the last verse of the song. The entire school was in an uproar, laughing about the dumb kid who had forgotten to do one thing—just one thing. This was the beginning and end of my stage career.

"What is this all about? Do you know the drinking water thing? Adding fluoride to our water?" Dad took a few seconds to respond and explained as he knew it. The adults were all in an uproar about putting this mineral in our drinking water. The water already had fluoride, but the government wanted to add more for healthier teeth. Some kids I knew were afraid to drink the tap water. Others would drink out of a hose and think they were safe. Okay it was me, but let's not digress, shall we? Dad said, "It was added to prevent tooth decay."

The story goes that it started out in 1945 in Grand Rapids, Michigan, making them the first community to do this. Now, in the early 1960s, there was still a noticeable commotion in states about this.

Some of the reasons or concerns was the fear of bone cancer in growing children. It was said it would lower one's IQ. I guess I would have been the perfect poster child for that reason. Anti-fluoridations also stated that it will increase acne and lead to Alzheimer's disease.

Dad just said, "We will do what the state tells us to do. It is good for your teeth as it helps prevent cavities, so you are unable to do this." With his tongue, he then moved his upper dentures loose and hung them out of his mouth. This was the first time I had ever seen this. My first thought was, oh my Gosh, my dad is a magician! I also tried to move my teeth out of my mouth, and my dad just laughed, and he pulled his upper and lower dentures out and held them in his hand. His face looked sullen, and he looked ten years older. At first, I was grossed out. I then yelled, "Ma! Ma! Dad took his teeth out of his mouth! Oh my God! Dad has no teeth!"

Water was good to drink, but it was always coffee milk if I had a choice. As kids, we would use leftover coffee. Then add a lot of sugar and milk and drink it over ice. But there was something even better— Autocrat coffee syrup, so no more real coffee to drink. I did not like chocolate milk compared to Coffee milk. Coffee milk originated in the Italian immigrant population in Providence in the late 19th and early 20th century when about 55,000 Italian immigrants came to Providence. It was an Italian tradition to drink sweetened coffee with milk. In the 1940s, Lincoln, Rhode Island's Autocrat Coffee, came into the marketplace. Now, it was the number one maker of Rhode Island's official state drink. Coffee syrup on coffee Ice cream or vanilla is pure heaven.

Chapter 10

The Age Of Reason

I was seven years old at the age of reason, and it was time for my First Communion. The Nuns prepared us every step of the way. I felt so clean and fresh in my faith, and I owe this to the Nuns at St. Kevin's. May was a good time of year, and it was not too hot to wear a suit and tie. We learned about the importance of receiving communion and what it means. Being at the age of reason, knowing right from wrong, opened new doors to being a new Catholic to receive the first communion. Knowing that God loves us and we love God and receiving Christ's body and blood would bind us more in his love.

The concept of becoming one with Christ and believing in His eternal life was explained until we fully comprehended it. We practiced putting our hands together pointing to Heaven. The nuns taught us how to make the sign of the cross. Sister Ann, my first-grade teacher, said it is like you are talking on the telephone. I heard that and flinched. Don't mention telephones to me! "So, children," sister Ann demonstrated, "As you make the sign of the cross, you are dialing the phone number to God." I wanted to ask, what if I dial the wrong number? But I thought better of it.

Nuns With Nightsticks

You could say it was like boot camp with all the training and instructions we received. Of course, you must confess your sins first to the priest before you receive the sacrament of First Communion. How many sins could a seven-year-old have? Oh, I had plenty as I relished in tormenting my older and younger sister. It was my job to toughen them up for life, and I was their brother. I took my role as a brother seriously. Hell hath no fury if someone hurts my sisters. It was my job alone to torment them.

From my first confession, I bet I have said a thousand Hail Mary's and Our Fathers over the years. I even questioned the amount I had to recite with Father a couple of times, but I never got the amount down. It is what it is, would be the response.

The funny thing is that, as I am writing this a few seconds ago, I looked at my bookshelf and pulled out my first Catholic Missal filled with Saint and mass cards throughout the missal. I received this and a rosary for my first communion.

Memories flood my mind, as I recall my First Communion. I am blessed to have the faith of a child then as I do now. Thank God for the Nuns; they prepared me for life. In 1962, St. Kevin's had only 18 classrooms for the first to eighth grades. It was a perfect small school to learn and grow. Nuns had firmly built my foundation.

"We are going where? Are you kidding me I shouted?" Mom and dad were just beaming and said, "Yes, we are going to Rocky Point!" Now, Rocky Point Park was an amusement park on the Narragansett Bay Shore of Warwick, close to home. It was only three and a half miles from home. It might as well be 50 miles away as far as my parents were concerned, an awesome treat for us.

I was tall enough to ride the roller coaster now! We had a bunch of cousins with us and had a great time. I will always remember my first roller coaster ride at Rocky Point. I was screaming and scared to death. I was sitting next to Sandy, one of my cousins. She laughed at me and teased me for screaming while calling out my name during the ride. She teased me like a sister, as cousins often do.

Joanne loved cotton candy, and my favorite was Dells Frozen Lemonade. We had lunch at the Shore Dinner Hall. It was huge and could seat over 3500 people at a time. We had clam chowder, clam cakes, and doughboys. We spent the entire day with family and to prove how much we loved it, Joanne and I threw up before we got home.

Realize that a young kid can be aware of national events, which in some cases, can frighten them into nightmares and stress. In October 1962, I was in second grade, and we were doing the duck and cover drills in class. Even as a kid, I knew this would not even help in the event of the atomic bomb.

We watched the film Duck and Cover with Bert the Turtle in black and White. It was a serious film, and the thought of an Atom Bomb going off was terrifying. The film showed two kids walking down the street and to 'Duck and Cover.' The next example was a family picnic, and they used the tablecloth to pull over them for safety. Seriously? I watched enough WW2 films to know this wouldn't work. Besides, I had seen the photos that were in Life magazine of the atomic bomb dropped on Hiroshima. People saved Life magazines back then, and Life magazine's one issue was issued in October 1962, 'Survive Fallout.' Even as a kid, I knew the 'Duck and Cover' drills were a joke, but they were done to make us feel safe.

The 1962 Cuban Missile Crisis was now in my world. We had a neighbor who built a bomb shelter, and dad said we would be safe as they would let us in. I did not believe dad because I had talked to the kid at the shelter a couple of days beforehand, and he said it was only large enough for his family. We were all scared during this time and figured we would take a direct hit. The Navy US Atlantic Fleet Cruiser-Destroyer Force was based in Newport from 1962 until the early 1970s. When they pulled out, the Rhode Island economy took a financial loss. The Navy War College was, and still is, based in Newport, so we figured we would take a direct hit for sure. We were all on edge during this time. I could not comprehend why these people, called Russians and Cubans, wanted to kill us and end the world. We heard about nine secret missile bases being built by the Soviets. Then, when the U2 spy plane took pictures as proof, it all became real. Adults were talking about this every day, and I became even more scared with the worried looks on their faces. As kids, we practiced duck and cover not just in school but also in the neighborhood. We had our run to places for safety. But not everyone showed concern or fear. Not the Nuns! No sir, they were strong and fierce, and you knew if something at school happened, they would step right up and handle that Atom Bomb. Nobody is messing with their kids.

I felt safer at school than anywhere else. The Nuns had a way about them as they went about their daily routine. We used to go to church every morning and learned the procedures of the mass. We would pray before each class started and at the end of the day prior to the bell signaling the end of school. We became part of the nun's routine. It is hard to explain, but with their deep faith and discipline to do the right thing every day was inspirational.

A nun could kick anyone's ass in my school, and we all knew it. They told us we would all be safe, and we believed it too. The nuns helped us focus on our faith and love of God, which gave us the courage to face the times we were living in. The nuns taught us building blocks on how to overcome obstacles and fear with knowledge, love, and prayer.

Chapter 11

Discovering a New Neighborhood

1963

I was not happy about the family meeting we were having. As kids, we did not have any input in the conversation. We had to buy into what my mom and dad were saying.

The family was moving into a larger home in another part of Warwick by the airport. Close enough to where I could still ride my bike to the old neighborhood, but that was it. I had to go to a new school and make new friends. I was going to live in a new neighborhood, and the loss of friends, school, and all the areas I walked and rode my bike would now be gone. I was born on Ithica Street, and now it will be nothing but a memory. I always had a sense of adventure, but my stable environment was always there when I needed it. Now, I would embark on a new adventure, a real one. I wondered if I was up for it. I was not all in on moving to another neighborhood at the time. I was against this, but I had no choice in the matter.

We moved to Cole Avenue 2 years after the new airport terminal located on Post Road was completed. You could see the faces of the people on the plane as they looked out of the windows descending to the runway. These were all prop planes, not jets. No wonder we are in a larger house; it had to be a lot cheaper with planes overhead. You could also see the Passengers' faces! We always looked up at the planes and waved.

The house was a big ranch style, at least to me. On Ithaca Street, the house was about 875 square feet for five of us, and the brand-new house was around 1200 square feet. It was a huge house, for sure, and it had a garage too! To keep the peace in the home, dad converted the garage into a TV area and a workspace for me using a construction set. Instead of wood, the set was made of Styrofoam. I was not interested in making Styrofoam crap. What good could come of this? I ended up making a battleship from a two-by-four three decks high and put it in a pond less than a mile away. In five seconds, it sank immediately. I was horrified as I really thought this through and could not understand why it sank. Pirate ships did not sink, so why did mine? I took it home and pulled out the nails to use the wood for another project. I realized I had no concept of building things. Dad saw my frustration and purchased an Erector set. That lasted about a week. I was so frustrated and could not visualize or understand directions to put anything together. I felt like a loser, and I disappointed dad. But I knew I did not have what it takes to construct anything. This ended my construction period. My hands weren't handy, as they were only used for talking.

I would soon be going to a public school called John Wicks. It is located at 50 Child Lane, in Warwick, how appropriate! No Nuns here, so no more smacking for me. I would be free! However, I still went to Catechism classes every week. I enjoyed this, and it is like what the new Catholics take: the RCIA classes. RCIA stands for The Rite of Christian Initiation of Adults. A process developed by the Catholic Church for prospective converts to Catholicism. New Catholics must take the courses and instructions before joining the church.

We took Catechism classes at the parish. In these classes, we learned the Profession of faith, the sacraments, the Ten Commandments, and the Lord's Prayer. We also learned about all the religious holidays back in 1963, which meant Italian holidays and that favorite dessert I mentioned earlier, the Neapolitan Zeppole Pastry. One of the Italian holidays was Saint Joseph's Day, March 19th. Easter, we celebrated my birthday, remember? Columbus Day is October 9th. All Saints Day November 1st. Of course, you had the Sicilian holiday called Feast of Saint Lucia on December 13th, Christmas Eve with the Feast of the Seven Fishes, and Christmas Day.

Being with the Nuns just one day a week was like a breath of fresh air. I learned more under this format than when I was in St. Kevin's school. I excelled in the teachings of the church and loved it. Okay, I was a sucker for getting gold stars; there, I just said it. I liked to hear about the battles and heroes of the Old Testament and, at the same time, learned about God and his patience with us. It made more sense now to go to confession to stay on the good side of God. Better safe than sorry, as they say.

I remember asking my mom if she believed in God. I did not know what faith really meant—believing without seeing and knowing your belief to be true. She explained this and why she prays in detail. I asked her what if God does not exist are we wasting our time. She looked down at me and said, "Better safe than sorry." I got the point right there: don't hedge your bet. Dive right in; better safe than sorry. All I know is that I felt better praying and being in church, so I was on the right path. I just had a moment of doubt, which is very normal as children tend to question out of curiosity.

The neighborhood kids were not as friendly as they were on Ithaca Street because we were not born on Cole Avenue. The kids I would talk to always said how long the family was in the neighborhood like it was a major thing. Being new to the area made me different. I found it extremely difficult to meet new people. I was not good at small talk.

Fortunately, I had an older sister who could make friends with anyone. She was the life of the party, as they say. She was always a popular girl. This turned out to be a good thing for me. I asked her advice and talked to her when I was lonely. A real big sister, she cared. At home, my younger sister Joanne and I would hang out all day, and she would often follow me around. She was also preparing to attend John Wicks and enter the first grade.

We were growing up in an all-new world. We all had to make sacrifices, and this is how I got a grip on things. Life certainly does not stand still. Moving away from Ithica Street made me realize just how good I had it. Now, I had to start all over again. It was a new adventure, but this time it was real. I had to accept these changes for me and my family.

We had a ball field close to the house, so I played ball every day: pickup games and little league. I would go and try to get some pickup games, and when no one was around, I practiced my hitting. A kid showed me how it is done. Throw up the ball in the air facing the backstop and hit the ball hard, placing the ball in 3 sections of the backstop. The bottom section would be a single, the next section a double, and the top a triple. If you hit it over the backstop, it would be a home run, but you had to run to go and get the ball. It was fun, and I was good at placing the ball.

I carried my glove, ball, and bat when I went to the field. My favorite bat was the home run devil, as I called it. It was black and wooden. The bat seemed to know when to hit the ball. I really think we became one at the plate.

One late afternoon, I was riding my bike by the backstop on the ball field. Six older boys were sitting on top of the backstop. Another kid pulled me off my bike and threw me to the ground. He then passed the bike up to the other kids. Then, they dropped the bike down on the

121

ground. They did this three times and stopped when they bent the wheel rims, making the bike dysfunctional. Several bikes were lying off to the side behind the backstop. All bent up with chains off the sprockets.

I went home without my bike. I was pissed that they did this, but there was no way I could stop them. My dad found out I did not have my bike. After questioning me about what happened, he said let's go to the ball field. I want to talk to these kids. I freaked out, worried that they would kick my dad's ass. I told him they were big kids and he needed to be careful. We went down there and retrieved the bike. Dad made all the boys get off the backstop and gave them a long talk about respect and honor, destroying other people's property, and how this affects the people they harm. Also, what happens to them when they do wrong and the consequences of their actions. I had never seen my dad act like this before. Wow 'Che Palle!" To me, my dad showed more guts and determination than anyone I had ever known. More importantly, he explained in the kids' language that what they were doing was wrong and what would happen to them if they continued this behavior. No kids would have done this in my old neighborhood. I realized that the parents around here did not monitor their kids like they did on Ithica Street. This was also an older, rougher neighborhood.

Mom instructed my older sister Mary to take Joanne to school and make sure she knew where to stand in line per grade. The same thing she did for me. Mary went to this school before she started going to St. Kevin's, so she knew some of the kids.

Like I said, Mary was popular, and when she got to school on the first day, she ran off to be with her friends and left Joanne just standing there all by herself. She abandoned my little sister! Joanne just stood there looking around, totally lost on what to do. Seeing this, I told the guy behind me to save my place in line and went to Joanne. I grabbed her hand and found the line she needed to be in. I asked what the names of the girls were in line and introduced Joanne to them. I was my little sister's hero!

As a result, years later, I decided to ask for a favor in return. Joanne didn't hesitate to help, especially after I reminded her of the support I had provided on her first day of school.

John Wicks was an exceptionally good school, but there was one difference. We never received homework! For a kid, that is great, but with homework, you retain the information better and end up learning more as well. It teaches discipline and how to study. These basic training skills on how to study and learn on your own is the Catholic School way.

I made a few friends in school and in the neighborhood with kids my age. Finally, I found them. The only problem I had was with the older kids. I had a problem with someone telling me what I can or cannot do.

I got in a lot of fights at school with the kids who were grades ahead of me. I

I managed to maintain my position but spent a lot of time on the bench outside the principal's office. The more fights I got into, the better I became. My best friend was Mike, and he was the brother of my sister's best friend Alice. One thing about Alice was that she was a little strange in one area. She wore the same winter coat all year long! I mean every day, even on a hot summer day. I always ran into my sister and her friends. I hate to say this, but they were the cool kids on the block. Wherever they were hanging out, other kids would come and gather around just to sit, listen and learn. They always had a few transistor radios blaring on the same radio station. A transistor radio was the first Boom Box, especially when you had more than one turned up loud.

Mike had a slender small build for a kid our age. He had blond hair and a big grin when he told a story. When he would speak, you would listen intently as he could explain things easily. He could tell a story so well you just had to listen and see where the story was going. We had the same interests, and our favorite thing to do was walk the railroad tracks. When you walk along the tracks, you see what most people do not see.

Ever so often, we would venture off the railroad tracks and discover new areas to explore. We always tried to get lost by going in a different direction and then find our way back. We would talk about school, church, and other kids in the neighborhood. We would sing along to Louie Louie from The Kingsmen or lower our voices and sing Ring of Fire from Johnny Cash. Our favorite was Six Days on the Road by Dave Dudley as we walked the tracks. Of course, we always discussed the TV shows we liked, and there were a lot of them—like McHale's Navy, My Three Sons, the Patty Duke show, and My Favorite Martian. TV westerns were awesome, and we watched Laramie, Lawman, Rawhide, and the Rifleman.

We both carried pocketknives, and when we found some good pieces of wood during our travels, we would sit down, whittle, and enjoy the day. We were not good enough to make anything; we just whittled. Mike would begin a story while we sat and had our pocketknives out ready to attack a piece of wood.

We never ran into anyone on our explorations until this one day. We could see eight kids down the track from us as we walked up to them. Each of them carrying rebars and hitting the tracks with them. As we got closer, we realized they were a lot older than us, maybe sixteen or seventeen years old. They were wearing dungarees rolled up like us. Hard shoes and white T-shirts with one of the sleeves rolled up with a pack of cigarettes in them. Each was dressed the same way, with flat-top haircuts. They asked what we were doing on their turf and that this was their area on both sides of the track. We said we were just passing through walking the tracks. They told us to turn around right now.

Telling us that it was not safe here; they were getting ready to rumble with another group. We objected to their demand that we leave as we wanted to see the rumble. Then they said leave, or we will make you leave. Mike and I looked at each other, shrugged, and turned around, wondering who do they think they are?

We never went that far down the tracks again. We decided to go in the opposite direction the next time. It would just be another adventure. All we did was walk a few miles, go left or right, explore, and then return to the tracks. We would put our ears down on the track to hear if a train was coming. We were always aware of making sure we could jump off the side of the track if a train was coming, and we always looked behind us just in case. We always stepped on the wood, never the gravel, so we would never accidentally trip. Looking back on our conversations, I remember that, without a doubt, Mike was a friend I could really talk to. He listened and always had good points of view. Like I said, his stories were the best. All his stories were not made up; they were told about everyday events that a kid goes through, but you could feel all the senses and emotions that he felt at the time. It was rather an experience that you were experiencing with him—going through an event in his life.

Chapter 12

Skirmishes and Tragedies

Next door was an older kid named Richard. He was two or three years older than me and had a friend, Lowell, who hung out with him daily. Richard was dark-skinned and was a little taller than me with a thick chest. I guess he was short for his age but stocky. He had jet black thick hair, not a crew cut or a flat top. It was combed over to the side. Lowell was a reddish blonde, messy-haired kid taller than Richard but skinny. He was weird and always said crazy things. He was a loose cannon, to say the least. They liked to pick on younger kids and fight them. Never one-on-one; it was always two-on-one. Of course, I did not take any gruff from anyone, and we ended up fighting. In fact, I would fight them both for several weeks every day on the way home from school. They would hide and wait for me in an ambush. I could always take one of them, but not at the same time. If I could take them one-on-one, then I knew they were not that tough.

Mike and I used to go to the new housing track about a half mile from our house. A lot of us Kids would go down there and play when the workers were not there. We played King of the Hill and fought each other like Knights with the wood scraps we would find lying around. Then

Richard and Lowell would come up and push us kids around to provoke a fight.

One late afternoon, when the workers left, Richard and Lowell came over to the construction site. Loud and boisterous, showing off in a threatening manner. Richard told Lowell to go ahead and do it. Lowell laughed and went to a house where the basement was poured a few days earlier. He pulled his pants down and, from the top of the concrete, sat in the corner and pooped. My first thought was, what an idiot. What was the point of that? They thought they were so cool. They were laughing as to which worker would clean it up. Mike and I were shocked and just shook our heads in disbelief.

The fights with Richard and Lowell were getting more frequent at home. I answered them back all the time. Mary found out how bad it was at school, and now at home, it was getting worse. It had to stop. They were older and bigger than me. I had no chance to stop it on my own. No way would I tell my parents about this. Mary must have said something to some of her friends.

Two brothers, Johnny and Jackie, friends of Mary, came to the house to talk to me about getting my ass kicked every day on the way home from school and now being at home all the time. I found out later that they were the toughest kids in the area, and they taught me how to wrestle and fight on the street. They had flat-top haircuts, T-shirts, and jeans rolled up at the bottom and wore hard shoes. I asked them why they did not wear sneakers. Jackie said hard shoes hurt the guy you're fighting with. Sneakers are useless if you kick someone. We spent a lot of time training. I wrestled and threw punches with each one at a time. I did not go in for the kicking part. I always felt that was the wrong way to fight— not right when someone was on the ground. I learned how and where to kick but never had the stomach for it.

One day, the two bullies were outside my house and had picked a fight with me. I did better with my new training, but they still got the better of me. Two-on-one was not a fair fight to begin with. Just when it was about to be over, the two brothers came. They walked up to the two bullies and asked why they were picking on me. Lowell then made a smart-ass comment, and then it started. I got to see a real street fight with kicks and punches thrown.

I mean, jump up in the air and kick the guy in the chest kind of fight. On the street—no less, there was no grass, so it hurt when you landed. You know what? Those two bullies never bothered me again. One thing about my sisters is that we are tight and always have been, and throughout the years, we have had each other's backs.

With my newfound training in wrestling and street fighting, I decided to go back to Ithica Street. I had a score to settle with a kid who lived two doors up from me. He used to beat me down every chance he got. He was a tough guy and knew it. Now, it would be my turn to settle things once and for all. I rode my bike as fast as I could and found him.

We had some words between us. I wrestled him onto the ground and beat him up. I then took off his sneakers and threw them into the 55-gallon drum incinerator. His mother saw this and quickly pulled open the back door and screamed, "David the Menace, what are you doing here? You moved away from here! Now leave and go back to your new neighborhood!"

I felt good about settling the score, and I indeed improved my skills. I rode away slowly with my head held high. I sure liked the name David the Menace.

"He is dead! I tell you, he is dead!" What Mike was telling me was unbelievable. How could he be dead? I suddenly became very aware of my surroundings; all of it might disappear as we returned to duck and cover. The Atom Bomb again! Hearing those words frightened me, and I felt lost and scared about the days ahead. Why, why did this happen? The day was November 22nd, 1963, a Friday, and JFK, our Catholic President, had been assassinated. It was around 1:36 pm on the East Coast when the national news broadcast the event. In school, we just sat there stunned, thinking about Russians and Cubans who wanted to kill us. A few days later, we all got together at the brother's house to watch the state funeral. His flag-draped casket carried on a horse-drawn caisson to the US Capitol to lie in state was sobering. It was the first Sunday after the assassination. I was eight years old and knew I had to grow up faster. Everything around me was changing at a rapid pace. The world appeared to have turned upside down and evil was around every corner. The sense of loss was overwhelming. Johnny and Jackie made sure we understood what was happening. They would explain in detail the news on TV and how all this might have an impact on us. How would we handle ourselves from now on?

Things were happening at a fast pace around me. We recently moved, and it all seemed so fragile with a new school and new friends. Will my world be here tomorrow? I wondered when the world would end. Were we under attack? How do you hold it together when you are so young to completely understand what is happening? You have no control or ability to change your surroundings. The only thing that stuck to us was fear of the unknown. Adults were in shock, with their faces frozen and still with the horror that occurred. Adults would whisper around kids, and we wondered why. All the private whispered conversations about what was next. What was going on? No adult would tell us. We just watched the news and listened to older kids explain our new world. We tried to understand, and we prayed every day and night that the unknown and our fear would come to an end.

One of the guys who was with us was around thirteen and could play the guitar. He and I roughly played and sang, "Where have all the flowers gone?" bringing us to tears. I liked hanging out with older kids as I learned a lot about my surroundings and how to handle myself in conversations. I was always referred to as THE kid. Did they not know my name?

We were all terrified as people were talking about who might be behind it. Was it the Soviet Union, Fidel Castro due to the Bay of Pigs, or was it the Mafia? Never ever tell me kids are not aware of National events that will affect them one way or the other. Kids are sponges listening, taking in, and learning from all who are near them.

I still remember the song lyrics from Skeeter Davis, "The End of The World," and that was all I could think of. The song went like this.

"Why does the sun go on shining?

Why does the sea rush to shore?

Don't they know it's the end of the world?

It may have been a song about heartbreak, but it sure applied to JFK. We said a lot of prayers in Catechism class during the first three weeks after the funeral in school. In my Catholic Missal, I found a mass card for John Fitzgerald Kennedy. The prayer was by St. Ambrose, "We have loved him during life, let us not abandon him, until we have conducted him by our prayers into the house of the Lord."

If I had been in Catholic school, we would have been praying about this every prayer time during this period. However, prayer in Public

Schools ended in 1962, so I could privately pray, and I did. As I prayed, I felt alone.

Daily, we would say the pledge of allegiance when standing under the flag outside at school. It meant more to us now to be an American. We came from different backgrounds and beliefs, but we were united together as one group that was reeling from the pain of losing JFK. We had one purpose, one goal, and one dream. Carry on what JFK started. Reciting the Pledge of Allegiance made us feel a lot better. We were stronger when we came together in large numbers. The historic words spoken by JFK became a battle cry. "Ask not what your country can do for you. Ask what you can do for your country." Americans will contribute to the public good.

We were all one in this country. There was something more important than each one of us. We healed as a neighborhood, city, state, and nation in time. We became a lot more aware of things outside of our control. I wished I were back in Catholic School, where I once felt safe under the guidance of the Nuns. I missed going to church every day and praying.

Because of all of this, I realized that I was totally wrong in my assessment of the nuns. They were so important to my well-being. Of course, smacking me around would not change, but like I said before, I could handle it just fine. I was used to this. I know that I was getting hit with the belt on my back harder and more often than I should have, but he was my dad.

One night, just before dinner, I wanted to wrestle with my dad. It was a challenge for him and me. I felt like I was more experienced now and wanted to fight him. He just stooped down and slapped my face on both sides when I went in to take him down. This went on for a while. Mom had enough of this and told us both to knock it off.

I went to my room with tears running down my face and working out with two five-pound barbells to work off the anger I had towards my dad for slapping me around. Later, I heard stories of my dad's father, my granddad, that he was totally brutal to the boys in the family. This explained a lot; in my mind, this was why my uncles seemed so cold and stoic. It was the Irish way, or maybe just my dad's family? I daydreamed of beating up my dad when I was grounded. I would have a surge of energy that would have to be released. For some reason, we never saw eye to eye. I was always wrong.

Chapter 13

A Series Of Dreams

Every day, I would lie in bed at night to sleep. I would see shadow men perfectly formed who would fight each other. Sometimes, there would be two shadow men, and other times, four of them. Suddenly, they would stop and turn to face me. Looking right at me, they started coming towards me. I was horrified every night that the shadow men would get me. I was awake when this happened and knew this was not real. But it felt real just the same. I could not understand why this was happening. I was too old to have night terrors, so where was this coming from?

I did have a recurring dream that lasted three days. I was being chased by a clown with a large knife in his hand. The clown was in the neighborhood chasing me down several streets. I knew he was going to kill me. When the clown caught me and turned me around, I looked at his face. It was the face of my dad. Weird, don't you think? I never went to a circus because of clowns. I wanted to punch clowns in the face. They did not make me laugh or scared, just angry.

One dream I had felt so vivid, it felt painfully real. I was being chased by a lion, and he knocked me down. He took a bite out of my side. When I woke up, I quickly moved the pillow that was on my side to comfort myself from the pain I felt.

It was time to join the Cub Scouts in third grade. Our den's mother was a friend's mom from school. They had a huge backyard next to the railroad tracks. One time, we went camping in the backyard. We put up several pup tents towards the end of the property and had two kids in each tent. That night, it started to rain slowly and steadily, then it began raining cats and dogs. The tents were made of canvas, so I looked up to see if it was keeping the rain out. I reached up and touched the top of the tent between me and the other kid. I noticed it started dripping onto the ground when I did this slowly. This gave me the idea to prank the kid next to me who was fast asleep. I put my index finger at the top of the tent directly over his face. He jumped up from a deep sleep to the dripping rain on his face. I did not tell him that it was me that caused the dripping water. He was pissed.

The morning finally arrived, and one of the kids opened small boxes of cereal for us to eat breakfast. We gathered around with our bowls of cereal and suddenly realized that we needed milk! We were all screaming about what to do. We would starve to death if we didn't get milk. The kid whose mom was the den's mother said wait a minute. I will go to the house and get the milk. Oh, yea! We are not in the woods; we are in the backyard!

I came home from a Cub Scout meeting with the big news. We were going to do a presentation at a hall in Warwick. We were going to dress like we were in the Crusades. There will be a first-prize trophy for the best original costume. I should never have opened my big fat mouth. Dens from the Warwick area would all be there, and there would be a lot of competition for the first prize.

My mom made my sister's clothes from clothing patterns. She was thrilled to make me a Crusader outfit. But she threw a wrench into the whole thing.

"I will not wear it," I shouted! "I refuse to wear it. No one else will wear something like this!" How can you both possibly think this is a good idea?"

My dad said, "Your mom and I agree that you should wear it, and we guarantee you will win the first prize for the best original costume." I was flabbergasted and outnumbered. My older sister was laughing her ass off. My younger sister yelled out, "I will wear it!" I was doomed— no way I could do this. I was to wear Mary's black leotards instead of jeans. No boy I knew would wear their sister's leotards. Mary added fuel to the fire when she said, "Be careful with them and do not stretch them out!"

My dad made the shield and sword, and my mom made the rest. I was good to go. On the day of the presentation, Dad decided we should walk to the hall instead of driving. Walking down the streets in leotards felt embarrassing! It was over a mile, and I had to carry the sword and shield. I did not want anyone I knew to see me. I looked like a dork in broad daylight with this outfit. My head was on a swivel, looking for anyone I knew along the way. We arrived, and I went to our den. Guys started to snicker and laugh out loud. Then, other boys in dens came over to see what was so funny. I ended up sitting next to dad in a metal folding chair. I just sat there most of the time with the shield covering my legs. Dad wanted me to go over and mingle with the other kids, but I said no, I am perfectly fine right here. My friends were already making jokes about the leotards, so hanging out with them would invite more comments directed at me.

Later in the day, we got up before the judges and paraded our Crusader outfits. Okay! So, I took first place for the best original costume. Mom was beside herself with glee!

I made sure I stretched the heck out of those leotards so I would never, ever wear them again! It felt weird being 'The Belle of the Ball!' I had made it to the Wolf Badge but was behind the others in the den. They had made it to Bear. I again realized I had no ability to make or create things with my hands. I was incapable of understanding how things worked. I could not see the result of a project in my head like my battleship sinking was my understanding of the physical universe. I had to use my wits, but I was witless at the time. I could not comprehend written or verbal instructions. It was like my mind would shut down and freeze up.

We had a family meeting, and we were going out of state to Maryland to see our aunt and uncle. Normally, we would go to Bonnet Shores in Narragansett. Dad said we would visit Washington DC, and Arlington, Virginia, before we went to see the family. Mom's brother looked like a younger grandpa: long face, light skin, and red hair. We would only see them when we had family reunions once a year.

I was excited to see all the monuments and buildings of our Nation. It was one adventure I will never forget. We visited the Smithsonian and spent a lot of time there, but of course, you can't see everything in a couple of hours. Still, it did excite me to learn about our history as a nation. The Lincoln Memorial was huge, and you would just stand in front with awe. Then, we went to the Iwo Jima flag-raising memorial. All I could think about was John Wayne in the movie Sands of Iwo Jima.

Along the way, some young men and women had armbands with SDS letters. This was the group Students for a Democratic Society. I asked Dad who they were, and he just said college students. There were a lot of people protesting on the sidewalks. There was a lot of yelling and screaming. Dad told us to roll up the windows and lock the doors.

We ended up at the FBI building to take a tour. Back then, you had a tour guide. I was the only boy in this group that we were in. The tour guide made sure I was right behind him. He went into a room and came out handing me a full-length paper target of a man with holes showing. I was so excited. I hung it on the back of my door when we got home. From that time on, I had no fear of shadow men. I had been to the FBI and had this target. Shadow men, beware; I know a guy from the FBI!

One of the popular kids' gifts in 1963 was the Easy-Bake Oven. My sisters made more cakes and got tired of it within 30 days. It ended up in the garage alongside the Styrofoam work set I had. Dad realized that I was not handy, so I got Play-Doh to see if I had any interest at all in using my hands. My dad enjoyed sculpting with clay and was skilled at painting. He also did a lot of drawings with a sketching pencil. I just made lumps with the Play-Doh and sniffed it. Yes, I really liked the smell of Play-Doh. I can smell it right now. The girls had zero desire to learn how to cook. Looking back, I wonder what our parents thought of us.

Winter is here! Snow days will be here soon! Every kid was excited. I loved snow back then because we got to go sledding and get into snowball fights. But the best was when we had snow on the streets. Automobiles at the time had steel bumpers to grab the bottom of and hold on. Cars would go slowly through the school zones. We would get behind the cars, squat down, lean back, grab the bumper, and slide down the street, holding on for dear life. This was so much fun, and it ended for me when a man driving the car noticed me riding his bumper and stopped. I ran off with him running right behind me. I could not outrun this guy. I ran into the house and went right to my room. My father was not pleased with that knock on the door. 'Your demon son is at it again.' I got the belt on a bare back that day. It was not the first time and would not be the last time either. I could take it repeatedly, striking my back. I deserved every bit of it, so I just took it.

We used to take our ice skates and go to small ponds. It was great fun, and the older kids would make a fire close to the shore. There were never fights or arguments. We just skated and hung out. We would sit and listen to the older kids. They were like adults but cool. You could learn so much by just sitting alongside them and listening.

One time, I went into my dad's drawer in the bedroom and took his switchblade knife. It had a yellow pearl handle and was sharper than what I was carrying. A few days later, dad was driving the car, and I yelled out, "Dad! I think I just lost your switchblade in between the seats!" I got a taste of the leather belt as soon as we got home. Like the Doris Day song, Que Sera, Sera (Whatever will be will be). I never argued with my dad. If I did something wrong, then the belt would come out. Hard to argue when you are dead wrong. He told me more than once to stay out of his drawer—guess I was just a slow learner.

When I was four, my mom was ironing a shirt for my dad. I went to touch the iron, and mom said not to touch it! It is hot. Then I touched it and yelled. All I could hear was, "Did I not tell you not to touch it?" I just wanted to see just how hot it really was, and I found out too, but it was painful.

I was in a lot of fights, and I was winning; I ended up picking on other kids older than me. Not just in school but on the ball field and anywhere I had a chance to mix it up. I turned into a bully and did not even realize that I had become what I despised the most.

My final fight as a bully was brutal. I went after a kid a year or two older than me, pulled him off his bike, and beat him up. I screamed and threatened him. I teased him when he started to cry. After the fight, I would not let him take his bike. I figured it had happened to me a few months earlier, so it seemed fair to me; I won. He threatened to have his two brothers come and beat me up, but I convinced him with a few blows that he should reconsider.

As he was walking away, I turned away from him. Suddenly, I was feeling faint and sick to my stomach because now I was realizing what I had become. I was a jerk, a bully, someone to be fearful of. I did not look at him as if he was a person. He was a challenge to me. I did not even consider how he must have felt being beaten down by a younger kid. I got down on my knees and started to cry. I was so mad at myself for becoming this type of person. I looked up towards the sky with my body shaking and prayed to God to forgive me, to not be this type of person, to stop picking on other kids, and not to be a bully threatening others.

142

"Please, God Almighty, please help me not be a bully again and stand up for those who can't defend themselves. Please hear my words!"

I then became very tired and weak. I got up from my knees, walked away from everyone, and fell asleep in the grass on the side of the field. When I awoke, it started to get dark as the day had left. Something happened to me. I was changed, and my heart was no longer dead. I stopped hating myself, knowing it would be a new day. I had a new job, and now, it was a mission. I will protect those who cannot protect themselves. I was eight years old and learned the power of prayer that day—the soothing sensation of the Holy Spirit throughout me. I figured just because I had a bad time of it now and then, and I should not make others go through what I was going through. I could no longer justify my actions.

I did not like living on Cole Avenue. I was in fights all the time. But now, I would stand up for other kids who could not defend themselves. I did not win all my fights, but I did gain respect. There were too many older kids with bad attitudes. I had to make up for my past mistakes.

Catholic School provided me with the comfort and the discipline that I needed. The nuns showed me the right direction. The daily routine of Catholic School and Church was lacking in me. I felt like I was just a leaf in the wind going nowhere. Mike was my best friend, yet I often felt alone and sad. I had to stay in my room as punishment for my actions. I had much time to reflect on all my failings. I just wanted things to be like they were. In time, I realized that you can't go back and relive your past— pretty deep for a kid. But that is how I felt. There was no going back to Ithica Street or the life I had known.

One time, I was sick with a bad fever. I was living in a dark, deep dream that I was an old Indian dressed in a huge, colorful headdress in a canoe covered with bright, beautiful flowers. The canoe was being pushed out into a lake surrounded by overhanging trees. It was at sunset, and you could see patterns of light over parts of the dark lake. I was slowly drifting in the dark, heading towards the scattered evening light, waiting to die. My eyes opened in fright to see the face of my mother. She had a cold compress that she kept dabbing on my forehead and wiping away the sweat around my neck. I will never forget the love my mom and I shared when we looked into each other's eyes. There is no comfort and love better than this. I will never forget that moment.

The only thing I did not like was square dancing. I couldn't remember all the moves, and I was constantly bumping into my dance partner Billy. Yes, we did not have enough girls to go around so Billy and I were paired up. We swore an oath that we would never ever talk about this to anyone. Well, times up, I just did. Billy played the girl part ha ha.

Chapter 14

A Journey Begins

1964

February 9th, 1964, will be in my memory forever. We were at my Italian grandparents' house on 111 Hendrick Street, a two-story home. Do you remember when I said my grandparents had 11 kids? There were only two rooms upstairs; the boys would be in one and the girls in the other. In each room, they had these huge air vents on the floor, and the kids would bend down, put their ears on the grates, and listen to their parents talking.

The back yard had a clothesline connected to a window on the back porch, so you never had to go out and hang clothes; just use the pulley and hang them or take them off from inside the enclosed porch. Grandpa built this huge wine arbor with telephone poles painted gray. There were three poles on each side supporting the wine trellis. The overhead was covered in red grapes that we were not allowed to eat. No sir, they were used to make red wine, and grandpa had a wine press in the cellar—no store-bought wine for him. Further back in the yard grandpa had a garden with rows of vegetables and a small grass area to walk on.

David Michael O'Rielly

I was sitting on the couch in the living room with 4 of my female cousins. Mary, my sister, and I sat in front of the couch on the floor. We were all watching the Ed Sullivan Show at night, and the exciting part was that the Beatles would make their debut. It was totally awesome until one of my cousins yelled out, "Oh! Ringo!" My grandpa came rushing in, thinking something happened, and he just smiled, seeing his grandchildren enjoying time in his home.

A week later, I was talking to this kid at the ball field. He said, "Did you see Louis Armstrong play that trumpet on TV last night?" I replied, "Nope, I knew he was in the astronaut program, but I did not know he played the trumpet either." The kid said, "I did not know he was an Astronaut." Just then, Mary's boyfriend walked up. He was clean-cut, wearing a collar shirt and slacks. He was a real nice guy that everyone liked. He never got into any trouble. When we asked him about Louis Armstrong and if he was also an astronaut. He laughed and explained to us that they were two different people. Imagine that, I thought.

March 14th, 1964, the Beetles were playing at the venue in Providence at Loews State Theater. It was on a closed-circuit big screen. My sister and her friends discussed going to the theater that night, and it would be fantastic. I told her that I also wanted to go but she said no. The brothers said they would look after me, so there was no reason I could not go. We were at our house, and everyone left to go home for lunch. Mary was adamant that I could not go but I was stubborn. She put me in

146

a headlock and took the gum out of her mouth, then rubbed it in my flat-top haircut. As I ran into the house, all I heard was, "You're not going, " screamed Mary. "These are my friends, not yours!"

I could not go now even if I wanted to. I tried to comb the gum out of my hair, but it would not come out. It hurt due to the comb pulling on my hair. The next day, I went to the local barber shop to have them get it out. The barber got the gum out of my hair and laughed at how ingenious my sister was. I am glad I did not know about tipping back then.

When I was riding my bike a few streets over, I saw this girl about my age. She was the first girl I had ever seen who did not have cooties. She was a petite blonde with short hair. I rode my bike up and down her street to get her attention. Finally, she came out of the house, and we talked. I think I learned about persistence right there and then. While we were talking, I noticed this other boy looking at us. He was maybe two years older than me. When she had to go into the house, I said goodbye and went to talk to this guy to find out why he was staring at us.

We started talking and soon realized we were both Italian. He recently moved from Providence to Warwick. I asked him where in Providence he lived. I knew the street well. I said, "Do you know my cousin Steven?" Remember now, I am not using real names, especially the last names. He said, "Yeah, I know him well. We used to hang out all the time around Mount Pleasant Avenue." Right there, we would have

147

no problems. My cousin was a leader on that street. He said I can't fight you over this girl because you're Steven's cousin. I was so relieved that I had to bite my upper lip to hide my feelings. We both agreed that it was best to walk away since we both liked her. She would not get in the way of my new friendship and cousin. That is one thing about living in a small state. There is always someone you know.

"Are you serious? We are having another family meeting. What is going on now?" I asked. We were all sitting at the kitchen table with wonder on our faces. This time, it was serious, so my dad went through everything. He said his company was bought out, and he has an opportunity to transfer to St. Louis, Missouri, and work for this new company. If we stay, he will have to work two jobs, and his mom will have to return to work.

When my dad would be laid off, my mom would go out and get a job in retail. My father had great skills and came in handy when he would be out of work. The one job he performed was as a court reporter. I used to play with his shorthand machine, but it had no markings on the keys. The Underwood typewriter had markings on the keys but not this. Dad showed me what the printout looked like. I was impressed by his ability to do this and what a memory to know what each key meant.

My dad was very serious, and my mom was nervous. We were going to move out west. Dad said we would go in a covered wagon. I did not know he was referencing the Rambler Station Wagon. I thought, how cool, just like the TV show Wagon Train, we will see Indians along the way. I found out the Indians would not be waiting for us.

Mom and dad would fly out to Saint Louis, look for a home to purchase, and then come back and get us. This made no sense to me. I did not realize this would be in another state. Dad had to get a map out and show us where Missouri was. We were ending up smack dab in the middle of the United States. Good, get me out of this neighborhood and make a fresh start. I was getting used to the idea of starting over in a new place. I was up for it. It all sounded so good until mom's family realized their sister would be moving away. That is when I realized I would no longer see my family again. Dad assured us we would come back home for two weeks every year and see both sides of the family. The move to the new land in the Midwest strengthened my bond with my sisters like never before. It was us three against the rest of the world. We were heading for the biggest adventure of our lives up to this point. I was still confused as to what states were. Geography was not my thing. Up until now, I had always thought Rhode Island was the world.

We spent the next few weeks with both sides of the family saying goodbye. Both sides changed the dates for the family reunions. This way, we would be able to go to each of them when we returned. I felt so alone, knowing I would be without my family. What am I going to do? We will be on our own—no aunts, uncles, or cousins to visit and hang out with.

And I was just getting used to talking and staying connected through the phone; now I was worried.

Mom and dad returned from St. Louis with some great news. We would drive out to our new home and school in a few weeks. Our home would be in a suburb called Crestwood, and there was a Catholic school within walking distance of our home. Further up the street was the mall. Also, within a half mile were two grocery stores, a movie theater, a drive-in, a fire, and a police department. I will be able to go anywhere I need to go on my bike.

After saying goodbye to family and friends, it was a sorrowful time for all of us. But we also had an adventure coming our way, and we were excited and a little apprehensive.

Chapter 15
Summers of Change

We drove, and it took us three whole days to ask if we were there yet. We stayed two weeks at the Holiday Inn until we could move into our home. We swam at the pool every day and forgot about the new home and school. We were in the middle of summer and getting used to the HUMIDITY! I could write a chapter on humidity in St. Louis—dripping sweat, clothes sticking to your body, and heavy air to breathe in. What a culture shock! There was no ocean breeze to cool you down.

We entered the new home, and it had a carport instead of a garage. It was 1,212 square feet, and it seemed huge to us. But it had no basement, and we knew nothing about tornadoes. Saint Louis County did not get a warning siren until 1967 after a severe tornado hit the county, claiming three lives and injuring 216 people. The weather service did not know there was a tornado until after it ran its course. Three days after the tornado struck, the Chief Meteorologist at the Weather Bureau called for civil air raid sirens to be utilized to send tornado warnings.

When the movers came and the house was set up well, we left the hotel to go home. My older sister and I stood looking at the shower in the bathroom. It was like a hotel with a shower. We had never seen a shower in a house before. The shower was always outside and was used to get the sand off from going to the beach. It was so hot people told us you could fry an egg on the pavement. It's not quite the analogy that you could fry a frittata!

We were excited that the family next door was half Italian and had 7 kids from Mary's to Joanne's age. Perfect for us being new to the neighborhood. We realized that the people in St. Louis talked funny and were difficult to understand. It was like another world. I could not understand why people talked with this weird accent. Also, they did not like the Red Sox! I knew I could no longer wear my Red Sox cap. I was very sad and felt I was betraying the team.

I wore sneakers, not tennis shoes. I used elastics, not rubber bands. I would get a drink from the bubbler, which is pronounced bubblah, not the water fountain. I remember the kid next door asked if I wanted a pop. I said no, I did not need to talk to your dad. He said not my dad, do you want a pop? You mean soda? I call them fireflies, not lightning bugs. Tomato sauce with meat juices from the meatballs or sausage is gravy, but in St. Louis, it was all just tomato sauce. A shopping cart back in Warwick was a carriage. We ate grinders, not subs. You say fire hydrant, and I say fireplug. It is a lollipop, don't call me a sucker! We had yard sales, not garage sales, because the car is in the garage! I knew we were living in another world. What was this, the Bizarro Superman world?

The St. Louis baseball Cardinals were now going to be my home team. No longer would I be able to watch the Boston Red Sox. I was devastated, to say the least. Goodbye Yaz; I will remember you forever. I was now learning about the National League. We received two papers a day, morning and evening. I always grabbed the sports page and read it before dad came home. I had a lot to learn about the National League, learning new teams, players, and box scores. When dad came home from work no one would speak to him. He had to unwind from a hard day at work. Mary would make his Presbyterian and put it gently on a coaster in front of him. I would refold the paper with the sports page in it and put the paper in front of him as he sat at the table. Joanne would get his slippers as the last act before dinner, then carry his shoes back to his bedroom. The three of us would then disappear and not make a sound until mom called us for dinner. It was the private time for mom and dad to discuss the day and hopefully not be about me.

Mom got the idea of putting a weekly calendar on the refrigerator to indicate what we would have for dinner each night. She got tired of having four people walk up to her each day and ask, "What's for dinner?" Dad mentioned more than once that mom was not a short-order cook, and if we did not eat what was put in front of us, we could go to our room without dinner. Mom, of course, would sneak us dinner, but you never knew for sure. On Monday nights, there was always spaghetti and meatballs. It was pork chops on Wednesday, and Saturday was dad's night to cook and it was always breakfast food. Tuesday, Thursday, and Friday were mystery meals, and mom would try something different. I remember mom pulled a tray out of the oven. "Here you go, pigs in a blanket." I replied, "That is a hot dog, not a pig." We ate at 3 pm on Sunday, and there was always a feast. We would eat, talk, take a break, and eat some more—a little taste of Italy.

The only time mom got a little creative in preparing a meal came on a dark winter's night. She got the idea to really try something different. It was Chinese food, and we had never eaten Chinese food before. None of us had ever eaten a fortune cookie. It was canned Chow mein, using bean sprouts and celery trimmings. The noodles were separate from the Vegetables. It was the Chun King brand.

Luigino Jeno Paulucchi was of Italian ancestry and served in Asia during World War 2 and started the Chung King corporation as well as Jeno's Pizza Rolls. I mean, we ate American Chop Suey, so we thought it might be the same thing—American Chop Suey as it was known in New England. In other areas of the country, it would be called American Goulash. A similar dish would be Beefaroni, and I am not going there with that version of so-called food. Chef Boyardee made it, and you had to hear that song playing in your head for days. "We're having Beefaroni, Beef, and macaroni. Beefaroni's full of meat, Beefaroni's really neat, Beefaroni's fun to eat, Hooray for Chef Boyardee!"

Now, we always have staples in the house. We would have frittata served at room temperature. Mom would make wine and pepper biscotti, which was literally to die for. Not to mention, we always had chocolate chip, peanut butter, and oatmeal cookies on hand.

When I first met the kid around my age next door, I walked up to the boy named Johnny and asked him one simple question. "Who do I have to fight to make my place in the gang?" Johnny looked at me blankly and said, "Gang? We do not have a gang around here." I looked confused and said, "No gang? Then how do you protect yourself or stop other kids from coming into your neighborhood?" He did not understand the culture where I came from. I thought they must be a different type of Italian, maybe another part of Italy. Johnny said, "Anyone can walk into our neighborhood, and we don't care." May wonders never cease.

I mentioned that he talked funny, and he said we are normal around here, and you're the one who is talking funny. I would pronounce car like caar. The end of the words would lift in tone, typical New England sounding, from Providence. He did not speak with his hands as I did. It took a while to feel each other out. I left a few minutes after that and went into my room. I sat there wondering about all the differences between Crestwood and Warwick. I was in a strange new world and everything around me was different. It was not a bad different, simply different.

We had been in the house for a few weeks and my older sister decided we needed to have a family meeting at the very moment. Mary was pissed off about something. I did not know that as kids we could call a family meeting. To me, this was a mutiny in the family. Mary made sure we were gathered at the kitchen table before she began to speak.

"Mom and Dad, it is now August here in St. Louis, and none of us can stay outside for more than 15 minutes before we have a heat stroke." She firmly stated, a little over the top, that it was about 15 minutes, but I got the point. It was like 95 degrees with extremely high humidity. I had to come home one day because I had a heat stroke and passed out. It was miserable and I wondered, how does Tarzan do it? Mary was right; we needed help. "Dad, we need air conditioning like the other families around here. It is miserable here, and at night, we are unable to sleep." Dad mentioned the fact that no one we knew had air conditioning in Rhode Island so why here? Mary was going to get her point across one way or the other. "Dad, we do not live by the ocean with the ocean breeze, and it cools down at night in Rhode Island." She was on a roll. I agreed and thought, man, she was good.

The solution for 1964 was an attic fan as it helped. However, not at night with the warm air circulating around the house. It was so hot I thought I might bake myself into the Pillsbury Dough Boy! I did not have enough meat on my bones to be light and fluffy, but I sure felt that way. It was so hot you would find dead worms dried out while trying to cross the road. It was so hot I was sure that if a chicken crossed the road, it would turn into a fried chicken on a plate before that chicken saw the other side.

One of the great things was the Chase Park Plaza Hotel located in the Central West End In St. Louis. It was Wrestling at the Chase. This show ran from 1959 until 1983. The St. Louis Wrestling Club promoted the matches. They were a member of the National Wrestling Alliance. Everyone I knew watched this program with entire families enjoying the ruckus. In school, every Monday, every child would discuss the matches. You had the greats like Harley Race, who was from Missouri. Dick the Bruiser was my favorite, and I saw him on TV in Rhode Island. Gene Kiniski was from Canada—finally, the favorite of fans, the great Lou Thesz.

Joe Garagiola was the first commentator. Joe was a former professional baseball player. His position was a catcher, and he had played for the St. Louis Cardinals during the 1946 World Series. St. Louis won in seven games against the Boston Red Sox. It was Boston's second trip to the World Series since 1918. I read up on this series since it was against my former team.

There were so many players in this series that went on to the Hall Of Fame in Cooperstown. For St. Louis, it was Stan the Man Musial, Red Shoendienst, and Enos Slaughter. It was Joe Cronon, Bobby Doerr, and the great Ted Williams for Boston. Arguably, it is one of the best World Series ever.

I went with my dad to where he worked in the city. It was a Saturday, and he wanted me to see where he had to go and the building he worked in. It was a cool drive from the suburbs to the city, and there was so much to see and observe. I asked him why a lot of the windows were broken, and he replied that the kids did it and there was no way to stop them. A year later, his company moved right down the street from us on Reco Drive. The funny thing is that all the people at work thought my dad had inside information on where the company was moving to so that he could purchase a house close to the plant. He denied that he knew about the move, but his two bosses also transferred from Rhode Island, and I am sure they gave him a heads-up. You could walk to church and the plaza and now to work as well. Everything was now at a walking distance which made it convenient for us. Dad impressed me with how shrewd he was, and he could keep his mouth shut.

In the neighborhood, my favorite game was called Kick the Can. We would set a coffee can upside down on the edge of the next-door neighbor's driveway. One person would be 'it,' and the other kids would run and hide. The person who was 'it' would run and find one of the kids hiding. Then, they would both run back to the can to see who would kick the can first. If the person who was it kicked the can first, they would run and hide. Playing for the first time, I sure wanted to win. I did not know entering someone's outside shed wasn't cool. I was there for the longest time. The other kids thought I went home. Maybe I should wear a watch, I thought. But I was not into time back then.

Another game was 4 square we played with a basketball. We would do this to warm up before a serious game of horse. Other games in warm weather were dodgeball, badminton, Freeze tag, and croquet. We had a baseball field on Reco Drive that we could walk to. They had Koury League games played there. We would have pick-up games when the league was not scheduled to play.

A few more weeks went by, and Mary had been listening to my mom cry at night. Mom missed the family, simple as that. She had never moved away from Rhode Island before. Mary sent a letter to my Aunt Mary. Again, there were so many aunts named Mary, and it was hard to keep up; welcome to my world. This upset the family back home, making them realize mom needed them. That is when, out of the blue, Uncle Peter and Aunt Mary just showed up at our house. We had no idea they would be coming. It was a pleasant surprise. This holiday was better than any other holiday we have had till now. We had family to see us in St. Louis, and we understood the words coming out of their mouths! They stayed a week, and we showed them around St. Louis and what our daily routine was like. Thanks to my sister, Summer ended on a great note, and mom was back to her old self again.

Chapter 16

Consequences and Corrections

Summer was coming to an end and that meant going back to school. The school was at the top of Sappington Road, and we lived off Rayburn on Aloha Drive. The Catholic school was called St. Elizabeth's of Hungry. I did not know there was a Saint for hungry people. This school's uniform was a white shirt, red tie, and black pants. I was looking forward to going back to Catholic school. I knew I needed it for all areas of my life. Even a child knows that they'll be screwed up. Luckily, I knew how Catholic schools operate, so I didn't dread the first day of school. The three of us dressed, ate some coco puffs and went on our short walk to school. For once, I was excited to go to school. I missed and needed the routine.

I was finishing 3rd grade and heading into 4th grade. I did not notice then and never really thought about it, but I was behind everyone in reading, writing, and arithmetic. I scored okay in my previous school, but now it was all different. I was back in Catholic School, where it was a lot more difficult. But on the first day, I figured I knew what this school would be like. The three of us found our grades and got in line for the Pledge of Allegiance. Then we entered the new school, and in my class, I was introduced. Not too many kids had heard of Rhode Island, and some did not even know it was a state. I was a new kid again, and it was not a problem until I opened my mouth. The kids said I talk funny and teased me about my accent. This was ongoing every day, all day long.

I was also being teased because of my freckles. Apparently, I had more than most people. The teasing and constant mentioning of the freckles made me self-conscious. I was watching Leave it to Beaver, and this one episode had him in the same situation as me. Imagine that bullying was such a serious issue that it was being highlighted on TV. I watched to see what Beaver would do to find a solution. He went out to the garage to get sandpaper to take the freckles off his face. Right after watching this, I ran out to the carport where my dad had his tools. I grabbed some sandpaper and worked on my face. I rubbed my face raw, and it hurt at just the touch of it. When the redness wore off, the freckles were still there. You got to be kidding me, I thought. What did I do wrong? Years later, I watched the same episode, but I watched the entire show this time. It did not work for him either. He got the same result as me. That's what I get for leaving the show too early.

The teasing continued for a few weeks, and I had enough of it. The main instigator was a kid about my size. I took him on, but I lost it. I guess with all the teasing, I just kept it inside. Then I exploded into a rage of anger. We pushed each other, and both threw a few punches.

I got him down on the ground and got on top of him. I grabbed his head with both hands and began banging it on the pavement right in front of the school. I did not remember any of this right after it happened. Johnny, who was watching, told me later. He was a year behind me in third grade. The kid's older brother had to pull me off. It never happened before where I could not remember a fight. I blacked out and saw red. That's the only way to really explain it. Maybe I was getting a little Vinny Testosterone going through my body. I never had so much energy inside of me, and it was overwhelming. I guess this might explain the tears that were flowing down my face. It was like an emotional waterfall. I had won the fight but lost control, and that scared me.

The only good thing after the fight was that the teasing stopped. The bad thing was meeting Mother Superior for the first time. I was taller than her and she was a lot older. I heard kids say she was around when Mosses brought the tablets down from the mountain. I thought it was true at the time. It turns out she always had a couple of nuns around her when she had to lower the boom. Those two nuns would handle the punishment while she watched.

We had these small square windows on each door to the classrooms. She would tap the window for a nun to come out. That is when you knew someone was about to get it. This day, it would be me. I was requested to go out to the hall and meet the Mother Superior. She looked up at me and pushed me against the wall. Two sisters were on each side of me, holding my arms down.

"You are new to this school, and now it appears you like to fight. You like to fight, don't you?"

I said, "Yes".

She countered, "Yes, you like to fight?"

Oh great, she is asking quick questions, and I do not know whether to say yes or no.

"No, No, sister, I do not like to fight, I quickly responded."

Nuns are well-trained in how to trap you. You get so confused you do not know what to say. She looked up at me, and her tone changed to anger.

"Let me see if I get this straight. You said yes, you like to fight, but now you say you do not like to fight. Which is it? Come on, spit it out, which is it?"

"Okay, I like to fight, but only when I need to. I do not look for it."

"Look for it, what?" she smirked.

I swear she did smirk at me. She had me right in the palm of her hand. I had a hard time speaking with this move. "How can you talk without your hands?" She gave me a good look up and down while the other two sisters kept me steady, unable to move. Mother Superior said this is just a warning since you are new to this school. Blah blah blah. I

163

had heard all of this before. She turned away with a smirk so big I wanted to wipe it off her face.

I walked back into class, knowing from the looks of the other kids that I had a rep from that day forward. So, it turned out to be a good day after all.

I looked up at mom and said, "I'm sorry, I really am." She looked down at me with a fierce look. "Don't tell me you're sorry. You're just saying you are, but I can tell you are not! Now, who told you? Where did you hear this?" I felt bad and ashamed but could not tell her who, so I just made it up. "Kids at school is where I heard it."

She replied, "Then I will call the school and talk to your Nun, and you will get it again when you go back to school." The Nuns at St. Elizabeth's will not condone this behavior. What does she mean by "get it again"? What is she talking about?

Just then, she grabbed my arm and told me to go to the bathroom and put the lid down so I could sit on the toilet. She opened the closet in the bathroom and unwrapped a fresh bar of Ivory soap. I could only think of one word, CRAP! She held the bar of soap in her hand.

Mom said, "I will wash your foul language out of your mouth. Now open your mouth and bite hard on the bar." I bit the bar hard, and then she grabbed the other end of the bar. "I am going to move this bar of soap back and forth in your mouth, and you had better bite hard on this bar of soap. You will have shavings in your teeth and gums to remind you of your foul mouth." She grabbed the back of my head with one hand and the bar of soap in the other.

She rubbed it hard, and the shavings were all over and in between my teeth.

"You will sit here for 10 minutes with this bar of soap in your mouth. If you take it out, it will be another 10 minutes. I will be back to check on you."

Angrily, she stormed out of the bathroom. I sat there, knowing where I heard the word from. If I told mom, I would get it worse after dad will be back home. I heard this word from my father. But you do not tell on someone you just take what is coming. I sat there with the soap in my mouth, and the smell was so intense I wanted to puke. Luckily, she did not use Lava soap. I probably would have lost my teeth! Good thing I did not say Wop or Dago, right?

Pentecost Sunday is the day that you are confirmed in the Catholic Church. This is around the end of May or first week in June. In 1964, the bishop performed this. I was to be confirmed in the 4th grade. In Rhode Island, you would be confirmed in the Catholic church when you were in the 8th grade. This meant my sister, Mary, at twelve years old, and myself, at nine, would be confirmed at the same time. We had to practice the routine before Pentecost Sunday. Now, Mary was at least two feet taller than any of us in the 4th grade. She was in 7th grade, so she stood out. I teased her and called her The Amazon. I finally had an edge on her. I teased her nonstop every day.

My Dad's boss would be my sponsor, and as I knelt, I would have his hand on my shoulder. Back then, the bishop would go from one end of the altar rail with a kneeling pad to the other. One set of kids would go up, and then the next set. It was orderly and impressive.

In previous times, the Bishop would slap your face rather than shake your hand as they do now. It just so happens that I was in the front row sitting in the boys' section, and some friends and I started making jokes and laughing. Unfortunately, I caught the bishop's eye. We locked eyes, and I shut up immediately. However, as the Bishop made his way down while gently slapping the kids, they weren't the same for me. He hauled off and slapped me so hard I fell backward into my sponsor. He had to catch me and push me forward. The bishop reminded me of Mother Superior with that dang smirk. He knew I got the message, but it was not well received.

Dad got me enrolled in Khoury League when I was nine in the Atom 2 division. I would stay with this same team through 8th grade. The team's name was George Heating and Air Conditioning. There were a great bunch of kids, and the shortstop was the son of the sponsor and coach. The Khoury League was well-known and originated in St. Louis. In Rhode Island, I played Little League. Overall, the two leagues are very similar in terms of rules and the distance between the bases. I played baseball a lot in Rhode Island so now I could get back into the swing of things in St. Louis. This provided structure for me, and I loved playing the game.

Khoury League was founded in 1934 and incorporated in 1936 in St. Louis, Missouri. It is the oldest youth sports organization in the United States. The Motto of the Khoury League is "Khoury League is interested in The child that nobody else wants."

The positions I played were pitcher, first base, and center field. I ended up settling on being a pitcher. When I was not scheduled to pitch, I would play center field. Being left-handed provided an edge in throwing to the batters.

One day at practice, I got behind home plate to catch the pitcher's throws. We were just goofing around, and I was not wearing a catcher's mask. A foul tip then hit and fractured my nose. The manager reprimanded me for screwing around. There was no pain, just a lot of blood. I went to the doctor and got my nose taped up. Dad said I might look like Jimmie Durante after it heals. Mary called me Batman. I still played, but looked like a dork all taped up. Instead of receiving any sympathy for this, I was laughed at.

I also played CYC, known as the Catholic Youth Council, so playing and practicing for two teams took up a lot of time. Also, being a part of sandlot games, I learned a lot. Baseball in St. Louis is akin to religion. I was in my element and all I could do was think of baseball.

In October 1964, the World Series was about to start between the New York Yankees and the St. Louis Cardinals. All the games were at 1 pm Eastern time. Yes, all the games were played during the day as it should be. Not only that, there were no blackouts for home games. In fact, something wonderful happened as the first game of the World Series was about to start in St. Louis around 12 pm: the nuns put TVs in our rooms so we could watch the games!

Baseball truly is a religion in St. Louis. I could not believe it. In fact, wherever you went during baseball season, you would hear the KMOX 1120 am radio broadcast for the games. The signal could be heard throughout the Midwest with a 50,000-watt transmitter tower. The St. Louis Cardinals were one of only 20 MLB teams then. Today, you have 30 teams. With 20 teams, you could get your head around the stats and players and track the box scores.

I was not yet completely familiar with all the players who were playing for St. Louis. However, being a Red Sox fan and following the American League, I knew all the New York Yankees players. I had a few favorites that I was rooting for. The manager from the Yankees, Yogi Berra, was born on the Hill in St. Louis. Also, Clete Boyer played 3rd base for the Yankees, and his brother Ken Boyer played 3rd base for the Cardinals. This made the series much more enjoyable. I had baseball cards with Mickey Mantle and Roger Maris. They were so popular back in the East that every kid had them. But in St. Louis, you also had big stars like Bob Gibson, Bill White, and Curt Flood. I had the exact same batter's stance as Curt Flood—the American League versus the National League.

The kids razzed me about rooting for the Yankees, but a nun a grade above me, Sister Agnes, was also a Yankee Fan. She was from New York City and had a similar accent to me! She knew baseball better than me! She knew the Yankee players' players, rules, and stats. We would talk a lot during the series—Sister Agnes and I were against the whole school, rooting for the League and the Yankees.

I had a grown-up friend with two eyes. I figured out by now that nuns only had two eyes. We talked about Mickey Mantle and Roger Maris, and I showed her my baseball cards with a lot of American League players. I will never forget Joe Pepitone's grand slam in game six, where the Yankees won 8 to 1 what a game!

My new hero forever pitched in Game 7 to win the World Series. It was Bob Gibson of the St. Louis Cardinals— the great, serious pitcher who never smiled. He was all business when he pitched; you could tell it made some batters nervous. Despite being a right-hander, I'd stand in front of my parent's bedroom mirror and practice my wind-up. I wanted to be just like him. I'd practice scowling at the batters and mumbling as if to say, So you want to bunt against me? Bob don't let you bunt without getting beaned. Just call me Bob, thank you very much. Don't stand too close to the plate! Bob will brush you away.

Chapter 17
David's Ghost

Around August, Woolworths had a sale for a 100-candy bar box selection from Hershey's. Keep in mind all candy bars were full-length. Not the little ones they have now. Dad purchased it early for Halloween. I followed him as he attempted to hide the box. I sneaked around the corner on my hands and knees. He put the box on the top shelf in a closet where we had our dining room table. He moved it towards the corner out of prying eyes. But my eyes were always prying. It was too high up for me unless I used my tiptoes. I could put my hand inside the box and take two bars out—one for me and the other for Joanne.

Around this time, now that we were settled in and had established a daily routine, my mom began working in retail at a department store at the mall. Mom told Mary that Mary was the boss when she and her dad were not home. Mary would be on the phone as soon as she got home from school. We had an extra-long cord for the wall phone. Mary would sit at the kitchen table and monitor the hallway, living, and dining room. She would get on her high horse and bark orders if we were goofing around. Keep it up. I am telling mom and dad about you two. She was like a prison guard.

Innocent Joanne would distract Mary, and I would go get two candy bars. Whatever I could grab, I had no choice since I could not see into the box. This went on a few times each week until 4 pm on Halloween. Dad opened the closet door, took out the candy box, and had a funny look on his face. When he pulled the top of the box apart, he found only 4 bars left in the box. He shouted, "You damn kids, what have you done? Now I must go to the store and buy candy for tonight!" He rushed out of the house, yelling at us.

It was a week before Halloween, our first year in St. Louis. Mary, Joanne, and I wanted to purchase costumes for trick-or-treating. But mom and dad said no, it costs too much. "But we can't make costumes," I shouted. Dad instructed mom to go in the carport and get three burlap sacks. He made ponchos out of each sack. I looked at dad and said," What are we supposed to be?" Dad took a second and said, "If anyone asks you what your costume is, just say you are dressed as a poor person." I said what dad told me to say and received some strange looks at every house we entered. Yes, we went inside every house.

In those days, you did not receive candy unless you told a joke, sang a song, or told a funny story. You had to work for that candy. It is a St. Louis tradition that started in the Irish community. It is said that the Irish immigrants who came to St. Louis celebrated the Gaelic harvest festival of Samhain. Ancient Celts would dress up in costume to deflect the attention of ghosts. During the festival processional through the village, people offered poems in trade for food. Poems then turned into jokes, stories, or songs.

Later that night, I did not feel bad about taking the candy out of the box. I figured no costume, no candy. By the way, those burlap sacks made you itch like crazy!

Mom and dad became friends with a family up the street. On Friday nights, they would take turns and play cards at each other's house. One night Mary went to a sleepover, so it was just Joanne and I at home while they played cards.

My parents had a good setup in the kitchen as it had a pocket door for privacy and to keep the noise down. Then dad would shut the door leading down the hallway to the bedrooms. Joanne was sleeping in bed by herself for the first time in her life. She was nervous and a little scared to be alone in her room at night with the door closed.

That is when I had a great idea. About 30 minutes after the grownups were playing cards, I put my plan into action. I made ghostly sounds, "Wooooooo Wooooooo," and Joanne started yelling for Dad. "Dad! Dad! Dad! I would listen for the pocket door to open, and I shut up. Dad came down the hall, "Joanne, what is the matter? Why are you yelling?" Joanne was shaking, and I could hear it in her voice. "There is a ghost in my room, and I'm scared!" Dad said, "Joanne, there is no ghost, and I did not hear anything, so I went back to sleep."

Good, I thought they could not hear me in the kitchen. I waited a few minutes and started my ghost call again. Joanne yelled out, "Dad! Dad! Dad! The pocket door opens up, and I shut up. He opened the hallway door, and I could tell he was getting upset with Joanne.

"What is it now? Dad was angry. Joanne cried out, It's the ghost! The ghost is back!" I was lying down pretending to sleep, and dad opened the door, looked in, and shut it.

The third time I did this, I should have known I was pressing my luck. After dad calmed Joanne down, he left and shut the hallway door. I waited only a few minutes and did my ghost call, "Wooooooo, Wooooooo." Then dad opens my door. He was waiting for me to start it up. He just closed the hallway door but did not go through into the kitchen.

"David, knock it off and stop scaring your sister!" Joanne heard this and yelled, "I will get you back. You wait and see!"

St. Elizabeth's of Hungary parish opened in 1956, and here I am in 1964 in this new Church and school. It was not a fancy church or school but was a monument of faith for us. We received a lot of homework; on weekends, we would get three additional hours of study. It was tough, a lot tougher than John Wicks. Looking back, it was the best thing for me. In class, I would sit in the back of the room, and my grades would fail. It was bad enough to cause concern for my teacher and parents.

One day, Sister asked me to read what was on the blackboard. I could not read it at all; the words very blurry. Sister wrote a letter to my parents informing them that I needed glasses. Upon reading this note, my parents were insistent that I did not need it. When I returned to school, I told Sister that my parents firmly stated I did not need glasses. She wrote a second note calling for a conference with my parents. She had made it clear I couldn't see clearly and glasses were now necessary for me. By the end of the second semester, my grades had improved. Thank you, Sister! One thing about a nun back then: they always had your back in times of need!

When I received my glasses, I went walking around the neighborhood with Johnny. The first thing I noticed was the bright green leaves on the trees and how close the school was to our house. I could see kids down the street and knew who they were. The colors of the cars were so vivid. It was Amazing Grace. I was blind now, I see.

One of the kids in the class was a jokester. I tell you what, this guy was so outrageous, and he was funny. Well, we were taking the Iowa Exams, a standardized test. The exams covered vocabulary, word analysis, reading comprehension, mathematics, and other subjects to see how you compare with other students. Something happened in class, and all the boys were out of control and laughing. The funny man was Frankie, and he was on a legendary roll, and we could not contain ourselves.

Sister had to call for reinforcements and met them outside the classroom. The three of them came back in with a refrigerator box, took the box, and put it over Frankie and the desk. She told him to be quiet and remain still. It hurt like crazy trying not to snicker, and we were warned several times not to laugh about Frankie's situation.

About 5 minutes into the box, Frankie started to sing, and Sister took the pointer and banged the box, and you knew the box hit his head on both sides. Hearing him complain was like an echo, and she hit that box again to shut him up. But we could not stop laughing.

That is when Sister Agnes used the final solution. This was our last class of the day. Sister said each of us must put masking tape over our mouths. We could not take it off until we got home. If you took it off before you got home, then you would be punished in school. The kids on the bus wore it all the way home like I did walking home. Other kids were asking, "What is going on wearing the masking tape?" Only a muffled response could we muster. The nuns had spies everywhere. They would rat you out in a heartbeat.

You need to understand we lived in a Parish, and things were different back then. In fact, if a kid went to school and told about something you did in the neighborhood, the nuns would react with tough discipline. The nuns were the Marshals of the neighborhoods for Catholics. It mattered what you did inside and outside of school. They had eyes everywhere, reporting back to them on what was happening in each neighborhood within the parish boundaries.

Johnny and I were walking to school when we noticed a balloon on the ground. It looked different at the top of the balloon, where you blew air into it, and it had a larger opening. I guess it was sticky and dirty from being in the street. I picked it up, and it stretched out really well. We got to school, and before the first bell, we were hanging out. We were throwing the sticky balloon at other kids, and all the guys in my class soon got involved. A kid two grades up came over to see what we were throwing. I said it is a weird balloon. Look at the top of it. He started laughing and explained what it was. I still did not totally comprehend it. But I remember he called it a rubber.

One of our favorite things to do in the neighborhood was to walk in the sewers. We would enter a large opening in a drainage pipe that fed into the creek one street over.

From here, we would hold onto candles, hunch down, and walk under the streets in the neighborhood. We would lift a manhole cover, climb out, and be a few streets over from where we started. Kids from other neighborhoods would sometimes track us and throw rocks and firecrackers into the sewer hole to keep us from going out. This would cause us to go further or to double back, creating a wild game of hide and seek. One time, we threw cherry bombs and M80s into the sewer and watched the manhole cover jump up in the air. These two were federally banned in 1966. I wondered why they did that. I guess, maybe because an older kid in school might have thrown a cherry bomb into the toilet, and it blew up. I am sure it has happened more than once in a lot of schools.

Speaking of school bathrooms, they had a round water fountain to wash your hands. I had never seen anything like this before. You would stand there, and water would come out to wash your hands. But the water did not come out when I was alone in the bathroom. This happened several times, so I could not wash my hands. Then I was in the bathroom, and some guys were washing their hands. As I came up to them, they left. Then the water stopped. What in the world is going on here, I thought? Why can't I wash my hands? I am supposed to wash my hands but this thing does not work. Finally, I asked a friend of mine who came into the bathroom, and he instructed me to use the foot push bar. Do you mean that ring on the floor surrounding the fountain starts the water? May wonders never cease.

Christmas was not the same for me. I was growing up and wanted clothes more than games or toys. I mean, I wanted toys, but I knew I would get tired of them sooner rather than later. I stopped asking for toys for Christmas. My one regret is my mom used to come into my room and kiss me goodnight. But now I was too old for this and asked my mom not to kiss me goodnight anymore. She had a hurt look on her face when she walked out of the room, and I felt like a heel. I hurt my mom's feelings, and I felt bad as well. I thought affection from your parents meant you were just a little kid, and I wanted to be a big kid. But truly, I knew I was not.

Chapter 18

A Heart Warming Family Reunion

1965

I was fast asleep when mom came into my room.

"David, wake up. We need to talk."

"What? What is it Mom?"

"Rick's mother just called and said he is inconsolable and is unable to sleep and can't stop crying."

"What does inconsolable mean?"

"It means you need to go over and spend the night with him to calm him down. So get dressed, and I will drive you."

As we were driving, mom told me that Rick had found out that Patty Duke had gotten married, and he was all beside himself. I told mom that makes sense because he is in love with Patty Duke. In fact, most boys were at that age. I went inside the house and into his room. He was on the bed, lying face down, crying and sobbing. I sat next to him and eventually figured out what to say to him.

"I heard about Patty Duke getting married."

Rick mumbled, "I can't believe she did this."

"It is what people do, you know that. Besides, you're just a kid and could not marry her."

He turned over and said, "But I love her."

"Too late now. You need to love someone else. What about her cousin Cathy? She is cute, and I like her too. She is my favorite on the show. I like her a lot better than Patty."

Rick sat straight up and looked right into my eyes. "What did you just say?"

"Nothing much, just fall in love with Cathy. She is not married as far as I know."

"Are you serious? Do you not realize that Patty and Cathy are the same person?"

I said, "No, they are not; they are cousins, and that is why they look alike."

"You are unbelievable! Why do you think it is not the same person?"

I was confident in my knowledge. "It is because when they stand opposite each other in the doorway, they both mimic each other. Also,

181

the theme song says that they are identical cousins. That means they are two people."

Rick smiled, probably for the first time in hours. At least I was good at something.

"You're a dumb ass. It is a TV show, and they are the same person."

"You mean they are not cousins? Are you serious? Why did they say so in the TV show that they are identical cousins?" I was confused.

Now, I was upset that Cathy would no longer be in my dreams. She is no longer available!

We just laid down, two lonely guys, and eventually fell asleep. It was all behind us the next day, and we never spoke of it again. I still say Cathy was better-looking and had a better personality.

I was hanging out in the grass by the Convent with three of my friends during recess. One of the guys said there was a rope that you could swing over the creek past the trees. He took a different way to school when he ran across it. Now this was not in our designated place for recess. In other words, we should not have gone down there. We had a great time acting like Tarzan and swinging over to the other side and back. Just then, we could hear the faint sound of the school bell, indicating that recess was over. The last guy on the rope heard the bell, lost his grip on the rope, and fell into the creek. We laughed, telling him it looked like he peed on himself. He ended up going home for the day. No way, he was going back to class looking like he wet his pants. We laughed all the way back to class.

When we entered our classroom, Sister noticed the empty desk where our friend sat. Sister asked where he was, but we could not say anything because he was in the wrong place at the wrong time. We said he ripped his pants and had to go home. We always played rough.

This was realistic, and Sister did not think otherwise. That was one close call, but it sure was funny. The next morning, we gave him a heads-up to tell Sister he ripped his pants.

In August, we went back home to Rhode Island. Back then, you dressed up with a sports coat and tie when you boarded a plane. It was a big deal to get on a prop plane, which was not something everybody did at the time— a very special occasion. Dad and I had matching sports coats, ties, and pants. Joanne and I sat together, and she was in the window seat. We spent a lot of time looking down and wondering where we were. I thought the farm fields were states, and I told Joanne it would not take long now. It took forever, but this was our first time on a plane.

I was slightly apprehensive about flying since I watched a plane disaster movie a few days earlier. Just what I needed to see before I flew for the first time. I was scared to fly and tried not to show it. Joanne noticed I was gripping the armrest like a vise during takeoff and landing.

We landed at JFK and had to take a bus to the next terminal to fly into Warwick. JFK was like a city; it was so large, and so many people were walking around.

Everyone was in a hurry, trying to get to their gates. I purchased a 'Man from Uncle' book, *The Thousand Coffins Affair*, and settled down in a chair at the gate and drifted off in my imagination. I would occasionally look up and see people from all over the world.

After a while, I needed to go to the restroom. When I went in, I realized toilets were pay toilets, and I required 25 cents. I had to go back to the gate and ask for the money from my dad. He looked up and said out loud, "Make sure you make the most of it while you're in there." There went my privacy. I always made sure I had quarters in my pocket after that. Never know when you got to go, and you gotta go.

Los Angeles was the first American city to ban pay toilets in the United States in 1970. Pay toilets were banned at airports in February 1973. By this time, my Limbo training had enabled me to crawl under the stalls in most cases. At home, I usually read three books I borrowed from the bookmobile in the Crestwood Mall parking lot a week. I liked to read about the US Presidents and Inventors at a kid's level. Also, books about kids or teenagers, their lives, and overcoming obstacles were available. It was my way to explore within the comfort of my room. The first book I purchased was a hardcover called Gene Autry and the Redwood Pirates. We were a family of readers. My parents always had hardcover books on their nightstands to read before bed. Our family would sit in the living room on weekends and read for a few hours. We read in our rooms when the weather was too hot, cold, or raining. TV was not geared for mindless all-day viewing. With only 4 TV stations, there was not a lot for a kid to see during the day, so reading was for me.

When we arrived in Warwick, we walked down the plane ramp to the tarmac and walked to the terminal to enter the gate. There were no Jetways or passenger boarding bridges. Jet aircraft did not land at the T.F. Green Airport until 1966. As we walked in the gate, to our surprise, there must have been 30 or more Italian family members all yelling and screaming with hugs and kisses enough to go around. It was such a warm embrace.

I stayed with my cousin Steven at Sand Hill Cove in Narragansett, about 100 feet from the beach. We would walk to Scarborough Beach, where the teenagers ruled. Sand Hill Cove was mainly for families. I felt like I was back home, hearing the fog horns and watching the Lighthouse light at night. All in my comfort with my extended family all around me.

My sisters stayed with mom, dad, and my uncle Ritchie at his lake house. It was an amazing feeling! We were home again, and the two weeks would feel like forever, and I never wanted to go back to St. Louis again. I really missed the family. I would daydream that something would happen and we would have to stay in Rhode Island—or at least just me.

The food was great. I enjoyed eating clam cakes and clam chowder—my comfort food—as well as pizza and real Italian bread. On Federal Hill, you get the real deal. The rustic Italian bread has a hard crust and is chewy on the inside. Also known as (Coccodrilli) because it looks like a crocodile. In grocery stores, the crust on Italian bread does not have a hard crust, and it is disappointing, to say the least.

We went to my dad's sister's house back on Ithica Street. One of my cousins was eating a snack. I said, "What is that you're eating? It is right before dinner." He laughed and said, "Everyone eats Pickens." In Rhode Island, a snack is called Pickens. You can guess what happened when we returned to St. Louis. We wanted snacks, and we wanted it at that very moment. We had been cheated on and told mom and dad we felt that way. We figured we would guilt them into providing snacks. At first, mom bought fruits, but we told her that it did not count as a snack. We used to eat Bugles by putting them on each finger and eating them one at a time to make them last. I have not eaten Bugles since I grew into sausage fingers.

I asked my mom if I could go and see Mick. She said they moved across Sandy Lane to another home. I was sad; Mom looked at me and said we had planned on seeing them later today before we left. Mom explained that these were starter homes and people eventually move to a larger home. I guess that is what happened to us when we went to Cole

Avenue. That is when I finally came to grips with the fact that things in life are supposed to change.

Mick and I were all smiles and had a lot to catch up on. He seemed so much older now and was almost as tall as me. Talking about day-to-day stuff, I started missing St. Louis. So, I went into detail on my daily routines. This was the last time I would ever see Mick again. It was a great Italian family reunion that year. There was a lot more food than I remembered from the previous year. We were treated like they had not seen us in years. We had the reunion at Uncle Richie's house.

I overheard the story from one of my Uncles that the neighbor across the street was starting construction and had heavy equipment parked right on the street. Uncle Richie went to ask him to postpone this as he was having a family reunion the next week. The neighbor said that no matter what, it would start tomorrow and take several weeks to complete. Uncle Richie made a phone call, and all the equipment was moved the next day. My uncles laughed and said it was nice to have such friends. I initially felt sad knowing that I would not see them once the two weeks were up. I made sure to see and talk to everyone and enjoy as much as I could with each member of the family. From this day onward, I would never take my family for granted. I wanted to spend time with everyone.

Eventually, we had to leave, knowing it would be another year before we would see each other. I was very depressed, and I wanted to stay. However, I started to like living in St. Louis as this was our real home, and I had to accept this fact. I could go another year until we came back home to Rhode Island. Then, I would get my fix.

It is difficult to explain the feelings I have for Rhode Island. It is not just where I was born but a magical place with so much to see. The ocean and beaches are different than those in California and Florida. The State is indeed very small in area and population. But you would be surprised to find out you know someone who knows someone. It is like having a large family. For all the years, I have gone back and gone to the same places and some new ones, but it always seems new to me. Like I am seeing something for the first time. I have never felt this way about any other state. This is why leaving Rhode Island in all its magic is always difficult.

Chapter 19:
Altar Boy Experience

I was now entering the 5th grade and had my friend Sister Agnes, the Yankee fan, as my teacher. The friendship did not last very long, as I got on her nerves. My dad used to say I had ants in my pants. I was the fidget Meister and was always looking to make a joke or do something funny. I was the second-class clown. The first-class clown was a master of disaster as he always went way out there. Yes sir, I am talking about Frankie.

Mom and dad came home from a parent-teacher meeting. He said he signed over rights, allowing the nuns to hit me if needed. Just in case I get out of line. It was called Corporal Punishment. I wondered if older kids got the Sergeant Punishment. Hmm...

I was drowning in English class, where you had to do diagrams on sentences, whatever. I never liked figuring out verbs, adverbs, possessive pronouns, prepositions, etc. I mean, who talks like that anyway? Do you pause and think about which verb to use while speaking? Okay, maybe not, but you're not me. You are lucky if you know which there, their, or they're to use. I was used to saying Yous guys all the time. How Yous doin? Worked for me and still does. I was so bored. I mean really bored, and I caught a fly and killed it in the back of class. I decided to give the fly a funeral on the floor beside my desk. I made a paper headstone and funeral procession. The guys were holding in their laughter, and their desks were shaking. The shaking desks alerted Sister Agnes like radar.

Mr. O'Rielly! Come up front, RIGHT here! She pointed at the desk in the front row. The guy there had to take my spot. Right here in front of ME, next to Frankie. I want to keep an eye on both of you. She did not think it was funny when I told her about the poor fly, and I wanted to give the poor fly a funeral. I sat up front for a couple of weeks and calmed down as I did not have a choice in the matter. Then Sister said we have a guest speaker today. "Come in, Father." Father Ellis came in and stated he needed some new Altar Boys and wanted volunteers. Right then, all the boys put their heads down. All thinking, please do not call on me, please do not! When you say volunteer to a nun, she will pick the volunteers, and you have no say in it.

She took her pointer and picked four boys like a bolt of lightning. Then she said, "Oh wait a minute, Father, you must take Mr. O'Rielly." The pointer was like the finger of God pointing right at me. Why would she pick me? I thought it must have been the fly. My heart stopped beating, and I had an out-of-body experience. Crap, I am going to be an Altar Boy? The thought terrified me, and I could not stand the thought of having eyes on my every move as a server in mass.

Almost immediately, the song by the Shirelles came into my head. It was Soldier Boy. I changed the lyrics so it sounded a little like this. "

Nuns With Nightsticks

Altar Boy

Oh my little Altar Boy

I'll be true to you

You were my first love

And you'll be my last love

I will never make you blue

I'll be true to you.

I felt Jesus was singing just to me. I felt so special and wanted to be the best server I could be. I had a fear of people looking at me and being the center of attention. An altar boy? What do I know about that? I had to attend some training sessions. I learned nothing more than the basic stand and kneel here. We did not go over specific procedures. Probably figured we knew it already. I relied on memory, watching the other proven altar boys from daily and Sunday Mass. A couple of weeks had passed, and I was ready to be a server, or so I thought. This whole thing was getting complicated.

We used to wear metal taps on our heels, and it was cool when we walked. The nuns did not like the distraction of the metal on the tile floor and disapproved of us wearing them. But we did it anyway because it was cool, and the nuns disapproved. I never paid attention to the formality of the mass as I was too distracted looking at other people. I could not sleep at all on Saturday as the next day, and I would be one of the servers at the 8:00 am mass. Anticipation and nerves kept me awake, knowing that I had responsibilities to fulfill during the service. I would be the third wheel, learning what to do. Oh, what Saturday night was like.

I had a recurring dream that I would slip on the tile floor due to the taps, slide across the floor, and fall over the altar rail onto the floor. I was terrified; all I could think about were the taps on my shoes. That's not a good idea now, sir. But on my shoes, they stayed. After all, you only receive one pair of hard shoes per year.

We used to wear a black cassock and a white surplice. Not one time could you ever go into the closet in the sacristy and find one that properly fit. So, you had to get there in plenty of time to be the first to get the cassock and surplice close to the right size.

I had more problems than the taps. I was terrible at learning Latin. I figured out a way to speak Latin. Anyone around me would assume I could speak Latin easily. I just listened to the sounds of the words and mimicked them. This was foolproof and enabled me to bluff my way towards Altar Boy stardom. The only problem is that I would be a second or two off the mark of everyone else. Since Latin was no longer used during the whole mass, I assumed I would know what to say. I had to memorize the Confiteor, which was to confess my sins. Someone had to start this prayer before I could join along. The other prayer was the

Suscipiat. May the Lord accept the sacrifice at your hands for the praise and glory of his name, for our good, and the good of all his church. Then, I had to learn all the responses to the Priest's prayers. I was to speak clearly and accurately for the congregation. I had to do this close to the altar in the Sanctuary. There was so much to learn that my head was spinning. Server training was not the best. It was learning as you go, and the Priests would critique every mass and provide some guidance to help us wayward servers. You had to serve and be proficient at the low masses before you could serve at the high masses.

At this time, before you started the actual mass, you said prayers at the foot of the altar. Mass began when the priest made the sign of the cross and recited the Introit or entrance Antiphon, and you recited a Psalm Verse and the Gloria Patri. The readings and prayers were in an order that made sense to me. The reverence for God was clearly visible to all. You started in this order: 1. The Epistle is to the left of the altar, and a Lector would sing the readings. 2. The people sang the chants. 3. The Gospel could be sung or read at the foot space of the altar. 4. The Homily was given, and the people would recite the Creed. 5. The prayers of the faithful.

The five parts of the Catholic Mass.: 1. Introit, 2. Liturgy of the word, 3. Liturgy of the Eucharist, 4. Communion rite and 5 The Concluding rite. I was so lost on what I was supposed to do. When performing my first mass, I followed one of the servers. I met up with a couple of Altar Boys to learn the 8 am mass. I would be one of the servers in front of the whole school. We got in early to prepare. But one of the older boys said we were going down for ice cream before we dressed. I said it was 7:15 am and we would eat ice cream. They laughed and said there was a way to go down to the cafeteria through the back door by the Sacristy. We quietly go down there. We were eating chocolate-dipped bars.

I then desperately had a desire for a fudgsicle. The paper was hard to get off, and it was so cold. I put it in my mouth, and my lips stuck to the bar. I could not get the bar out of my mouth, and it hurt when I tried. The other guys were laughing hard and said it was time to go up. What? Go up? I can't go like this. I finally made it up in time to get dressed and be ready to serve. I never had another fudgsicle again way too painful.

Father Ellis found out that I lived just a hundred yards from the Church. He instructed me that it would be a good gesture to be the permanent server for the 6 am daily mass Monday through Sunday. Even to this day, no matter what time of the night I go to sleep, I awaken at 5 am every day. I did the 6 am mass for four years and only took off two weeks every year due to vacation. I liked doing the morning mass as it was just me and the Priest. A perfect time for me to learn and ask questions. This slowed my advancement until I got it right. The 8 am school mass and 6 am mass were not the same as the Sunday masses, with every seat in the pews filled to the brim. Every eye is fixed on you, watching your every move.

I slowly progressed in my training from doing the 6 am and 8 am masses. Now, I was going to work on Sundays, regularly serving two masses each Sunday. Mom was so happy that I was in church every day. I was so close to the church that if someone did not show up, our home phone would ring, and I was off to the races. To be honest, I started to pray more and felt close to God. The routines of the mass became normal to me, so I could focus on why I was there in the first place. Being an Altar Boy was indeed an honor, and I was absorbing all of it slowly, of course, but eventually got it. Well, not really.

I did have one question, though, that I never asked. Was it okay to take Communion twice a day? I took it and did not know if I was committing a sin or not. I did not ask because I figured it was a stupid question, and I had plenty more of them than that.

"Hey Joanne! Joanne!" I was so excited I just had to tell her. "Dad is putting up the badminton set on the front lawn!" We had just returned from church, so Joanne and I helped dad put up the net and the stakes. Unfortunately, we had a slight hill that slopped towards the driveway. I figured it was easier for Joanne to be on the high side when we played. It was Sunday, so we would eat around 3 pm and play for a few hours before dinner.

I noticed mom was putting out the good plates and silverware, so I asked her why the big deal for Sunday dinner. She said we invited a couple of people to eat with us. I said, what people? Who are you talking about? We ate Sunday meals in the carport in the spring, summer, and early fall.

Mom said, "We invited your sister's Nun and your Nun to Sunday dinner today, and they should be here in about 30 minutes."

"What? What did you just say?" I had trouble breathing. I was hyperventilating, and my mom had to tell me to calm down. "We just wanted to share a meal with them and get to know them better." I looked at her, raised one of my eyebrows, and said, "I have never seen a nun eat before. I don't know if I like this idea. Am I in trouble?" Joanne was letting me do all the talking and was standing so close to me we could have won a 3-legged race. She was nervous too, and was not the angel I thought she was. I was going to see Sister Agnes chewing food! I have never even seen her take a drink of water. Now they will be here in 30 minutes!

Mom replied, "No, David you are not in trouble. Just relax." I thought, sure, I'll relax. I'm not nervous, just out of my mind. It was a hot September day, and it just got hotter. I asked Joanne if she wanted to play badminton to have a reason not to sit and just wait. We were playing when the nuns walked up the driveway. Talk about sticking out! Full habit nuns can be seen from miles away. Now, I admit that I was a little over the top playing with Joanne. When she missed a shot, I would torment her, talking trash until she was near tears. The nuns were watching and did not like the fact that I was tormenting my little sister. But it just so happened to be my job as her brother. I must toughen her up so she can take care of herself.

Sister Agnes said, "David are you really that good? Why must you torment your little Sister?"

"I can't help it, sister. I am good at this game. It just happens." I was a stud at Badminton. I ruled the lawn. "Okay, we get it now. Why don't you take us on? Us two against you. You think you could play us and win?"

I thought, of course you're nuns. "Sure, I will go and get two more rackets."

During the heat of battle, I took a break and looked around, noticing neighbors from the streets standing in the street watching us play. At the other end of the street, cars pulled up, and families were standing by their cars. They were watching the match of the century. Now, to tell the truth, they whipped me worse than I did with Joanne. I was dripping sweat so bad it was getting in my eyes. My shirt was stuck to my skin. I was tired and out of breath. In full habits going after the shuttlecock, not one sweat drip could be seen on their faces. They were calm, cool, and collected. People were laughing when I reached out, missed a shot, and fell. To make matters worse, they started talking trash to me like I did to Joanne! Two nuns were talking smack to me for all to hear. "Can you keep up? Do you need your little sister to help you? Come on David, we thought you were good at badminton."

People were having a great time at my expense seeing the nuns, who were so athletic, whip me good. I thought, is it time to eat yet? I must get out of here. Then, music to my ears, mom said it was time to eat, and we stopped playing. The nosy neighbors walked back to their homes, and the cars drove away with a few car horns saying, "Great jobs sisters!" Not the stud I thought I was. No sir, not the stud. I was humble pie in the face.

I could not stop looking at the nuns eating. I mean, they ate like us, but it just seemed weird to see them chew food. They carried on conversations and were funny. I had never seen nuns laugh and carry on like that. They were normal human beings! You know sister Agnes was alright in my book. I settled down and got the courage to speak and have a normal conversation—friends with sister Agnes again.

Chapter 20
Reliving The New Hometown

In October, the Gateway Arch was completed. This was a huge event in St. Louis. This came just a year after winning the World Series, a source of pride for us as residents. The riverfront where the Arch is located was bustling with tourists. I saw the benefits of living in St. Louis and started taking stock of all this city offered. There was Gaslight Square, where big-name entertainers performed. The St. Louis Metro area was larger than the state of Rhode Island in size and population. In 1965, you had the baseball Cardinals, football Cardinals, and the St. Louis Hawks basketball teams.

We went to Forest Park, which is five hundred acres larger than Central Park in New York and offers numerous attractions. There were a lot of attractions within the park that you can visit for a full day. We may not have had the ocean at our back door, but we had everything else and more than we could ever see and do. This was now my home.

Back then, families would go to Forest Park and have picnics. There would be families all over the park. Mom would bring cold chicken and several cold side dishes. We would spend the day hanging out and running around the park. The St. Louis Zoo was also there, so you could park and walk around the zoo. Talk about being tired from walking and sleeping in the car on the way back home. It was simple and cheap because the zoo was free admission.

We were in the back of class, and three of us were bigger than the other boys. We took a short kid and picked him up to give him bear hugs. We wanted to see if his back would crack. Suddenly, the bell rang, which alerted us that the class had started. I had Kevin in a bear hug and just let him go. He slipped and hit his head on the corner of the metal chair that was connected to the desk.

Blood was everywhere, and he was whisked off to the nurse, then to the hospital for stitches. The janitor came in and cleaned the blood. We were all in shock, and I thought it was just an accident since he slipped.

Ten minutes after Kevin left, sister Agnes walked in and was in Nun Mode. This is when a nun is on a mission, and nothing can stop a nun on a mission. "Mr. O'Rielly! Come up to the front, please."

I slowly got out of my chair and had to explain to my sister that I just wanted to see if Kevin's back would crack, and if he hadn't slipped, everything would have been fine. "You are nothing but a big ape!" she screamed. "You're a big, big ape!" The kids in class laughed and she looked around the room. She showed a fierce warrior face.

"Not funny! Kevin almost had his eye knocked out, and now he is going to the hospital to get stitches. He could have lost his eye!" We all knew that was crap, maybe stitches, but there was no way he would lose an eye. But we kept our mouths shut. I looked at her and said, "Kevin slipped; that is what caused it."

It was not a smart comment coming out of my big ape mouth. With steely eyes, she looked at me. "You are a big ape, and do not think beyond this moment." She was just a few inches away from grabbing me and letting me have it. I had to be diplomatic, but I did not know what that meant then. Sister turned around towards the blackboard and pointed towards the front of the room where I needed to stand. "Just stand there like the big ape you are." I walked slowly and stood a foot away from the blackboard. When she wasn't looking, I moved my arms around like an ape scratching himself, and the room erupted in laughter. I stood still when Sister turned around to see what the commotion was. Everyone calmed down, and she turned away from me. Two minutes later I started Ape scratching again. The other kids lost it, and she turned around to me. I thought, just when we were friends again, I am now a big ape.

Sister Ann then directed me to write 100 times on the blackboard, "I am a big ape." I wanted to sign the last line by Tarzan, but I thought better about it. Maybe 'Magilla Gorilla' would have worked, as that is what the kids called me for the rest of the week. After class, she sat me down and explained why she was so mad and how my actions caused the injury. It was not Kevin's fault it was mine. Then I really did feel like a big ape.

A few days after Ape Man there was a fight on the baseball field. We all rushed over to see who was fighting. It was Johnny, my next-door neighbor. He never gets in a fight and never has any problems with anyone. The guy he is fighting is two years older and a lot bigger. I jumped in and pushed the guy back away from Johnny, who was on the ground after being hit several times. I then got in this guy's face and asked him what his problem was. He should pick on a kid his own size; now, he was bigger and a year older than me, but beating up on Johnny put me over the edge. It was not right. Just then, I get a fist to the side of my face. A great right hook, I regained my composure and tackled the aggressor to the ground. Wrestling moves work to get your opponent on the ground to make things even. Especially when your opponent is a lot taller, and this kid was.

While on the ground, both of us threw a few more punches. I had him under control with my legs and one arm. But with our free arms, we punched each other. Then, one of the nuns patrolling the playground came over and broke it up. She separated us until the bell rang a few minutes later. I felt good that I had him controlled with my arms and legs. He could not break free. But it was a tie, to say the least.

I went into class, and sister Agnes could see that I had been in a fight with my clothes in disarray. She excused herself for about 10 minutes, returned to class, and did not bring up the fight. I was shaking mad at this point. About 10 minutes before we were to be dismissed for the day, sister Agnes said the class had to stay after school. She would not tell us what we did wrong, but we had to sit quietly and stare at the blackboard. Keep your eyes focused on the front!

When the bell rang, I looked out the window and saw that kid I fought with waiting with three friends for me to come walking out. I thought great, He can't fight his own battles and must have his friends help him. I was on my own, and I did not have friends who could get into a situation like this. I figured when we get dismissed, it will be 4 against 1. Now, I must figure out how I can make it a one-on-one confrontation by calling him out since he has backup.

I will just shame him, I thought. They must have stayed there waiting for 30 minutes. Then they walked home, realizing our class was being detained for who knows how long. When sister Agnes said we could go home, I found out that Johnny's class had also been detained. That is when I realized the sisters got together and figured if we stayed after school, the other kids would go home, and there would be no more fighting today. To be on the safe side, Johnny and I walked together with our heads on a swivel, looking for trouble.

How you like that, sister Agnes and Johnny's Nun worked together to defuse the situation. The nuns had our backs! They protected us and knew we were in the right as I stood up for a smaller guy. I should not have been worried about going home because the nuns knew about the fight. If anything happened, they would find out about it, and there would be hell to pay. I was safe for now.

The next day, we had 4 nuns on patrol in the playground and field. This would not get out of hand. It was all hands on deck to protect the kids. From this time on, I have always told people that if they want to have a safe neighborhood, they need NUNS WITH NIGHTSTICKS!

I was hanging out with a bunch of neighborhood kids next door. One kid was on crutches and was sitting down. He kept hitting me with his crutches. I told him to stop as it hurt. He kept doing it, so I hit him a few times, and he hobbled home. The next day in school, I was called to the front of the class as soon as the first bell rang. Sister said, "Class, did you know Mr. O Reilly beat up a child who is on crutches? He thinks he is so tough. Now, why would he do this?" Wow, these nuns know everything that is going on. I can't catch a break. I looked down, then up again, as I felt I had the right to hit him, and he was warned. I explained this to my sister, but I had to go to the blackboard and write 100 times. 'I am just a big ape." I wanted to go to the zoo to see my new gorilla friends; at least they would understand.

I was getting into trouble at home. Mom and Mary always yelled at me and told me to leave them alone. Dad finally pulled me aside to explain why I was getting on their nerves. He said at a certain time of the month, your mother and sister and in a few years Joanne will have a condition called 'The Curse.' This is when they get agitated. When you notice this happening, the best thing you can do is to walk away and go to your room or outside. Dad said this is what I do; stay away when they have 'The Curse.' It usually lasts a week every month. The best advice I can give you is just to stay away from them and 'The Curse.'

A couple of days later, I was playing next door, hanging out in the basement. Jackie, the girl who lived next door, asked me a question.

"Hey, do you know what a period is?"

"I said yes, I do."

"What is it then?" She was half laughing at me like I was stupid.

"It is what you put at the end of a sentence." I knew what a stupid period was. All the kids started teasing me about not knowing what a period is right then. Eventually, I realized the 'curse' was the same as a period! Why didn't dad just tell me that?

I was tired of Mary tying up the phone every day. I decided to do some phone pranks, but the operator caught me. You would call the operator in those times to get the time and weather. I called about six times to ask the operator about stupid things. All to keep Mary off the phone. Finally, the operator called the house and wanted to find out what was going on and Mary took the call. The operator was not a happy camper being interrupted by a kid.

Mary looked down at me and said, "I am going to tell Dad about this, and you're going to get it!" She was still mad that I was on the phone for so long. Dad was going to be pissed for sure, so I locked myself in the main bathroom.

When dad got home, Mary spilled the beans, and I heard his deep voice as he approached the bathroom.

"David come out of there right now."

"No, I will not come out."

"You come out right now, mister."

"No, I will not come out."

"Why not?"

"Because you will hit me!"

"I Will not hit you, I promise."

'Really, you will not hit me?"

"No, I will not, so come out. We need to eat supper."

I came out, and sure enough, he hit me after I took two steps down the hall.

"You promised not to hit me!"

His reply was, "I lied ha ha ha."

On Sunday night, we watched The Wizard of Oz on TV. We had seen it before, but it was fun to watch it again with family. The next day, I joined a few guys discussing the movie. One guy said it blew his mind when Dorothy opened the door, and the movie turned to color. No longer were the scenes in black and white.

I said, "That is not true. The movie is in black and white."

One of the guys said, "No, it turns into color. What were you watching?"

I said, "No, it does not. The movie is in black and white."

He then asked one question that changed my mind.

"O'Rielly do you own a black and white TV?"

Oops! I quietly slipped away from the group when I overheard someone referring to me as a 'dumb ass.'

I resembled that comment. We did not get our first color TV until 1967.

Mary and I were alone watching TV on Saturday night. Joanne was asleep, so Mary said, "Hey, do you want to see the movie Psycho? It came out in 1960." I reminded her that mom said I was too young to see the movie. She said. "You're old enough unless you're afraid? Are you a little scary cat? Are you a scared little boy?" That was a double dare if I ever heard one. Is my sister daring me?

I said okay, let's watch it, and unfortunately, I sat through all of it. For the next several weeks, I had the curtain open so I could shower. After drying off, I had to take the towel and pick up the water off the floor. I was so sure someone would barge in and knife me ten times.

When dad had the carpet installed down the hallway, the bathroom door wouldn't close properly, preventing it from locking. I was totally unprotected in the shower. Mary got a big kick out of that. She also got in trouble for allowing me to watch the movie. Mom kept asking why the towel was always soaking wet when I hung it up. I had to spill the beans on Mary.

On Saturdays, Joanne and I, along with a lot of kids, would go to the Crestwood Theater. If your mom went to the grocery store called Bettendorf's, a local chain, she would obtain free movie passes. We would walk to the theater, which was located on Route 66. Now, it is called Watson Road, with signs saying historic Route 66.

We did not have money for candy or popcorn. Mom said there is money for a soda, and I will pop up some popcorn for each of you in paper bags. Thank goodness they did not have plastic water bottles back then.

The movies were old and mostly western. One time, a friend of mine and I saw a movie poster about another Western show that was showing right after the free shows. So we stayed in our seats to wait for the next movie. When people came in, it turned out there were no kids in the theater; it was all adults. So we moved to the front row.

The movie started out okay, but they sure sang a lot. I told my friend that this is a different kind of Western. About 15 minutes into the movie, we realized it was a musical. We both decided not to tell anyone that we were in a theater watching a musical. When the movie ended, we both decided it was very good. It was called Oklahoma!

I was watching TV when Mary came home from school. She started talking Pig Latin, and I kept saying, " Mary what are you saying?" This was going on and on and driving me nuts. She finally explained what PIG Latin was, but I could not comprehend it. I finally told her that I could speak Pig Latin too! Shut up!"

Mary always knew how to get me going. Like the time she came home and I said hello. She then screams out, "KAW KAW KAW." I said what are you saying? "KAW KAW KAW!" I looked at her and said you sound like a crow. She nodded her head and started yelling, "KAW KAW KAW." She kept this up until Mom came home. You know she did it again the next day. You think I'm weird?

Chapter 21:

A Game Without Glasses

1966

The time when John Lennon of the Beatles made the following comment. "We're more popular than Jesus now." I almost fell out of my chair watching the news. Yes, it was offensive to me and others that I knew. What was he thinking?

In an interview five months after that comment. John Lennon said, "Christianity will go. It will vanish and shrink. I needn't argue about that; I know I'm right and will be proved right."

We're more popular than Jesus now. I don't know which will go first, Rock & Roll or Christianity. Jesus was all right, but his disciples were thick and ordinary. It's them twisting it that ruins it for me."

Talk about firing up the Catholics! Due to this, the nuns had a hard time keeping us focused. We felt we were under attack. This one comment made during an interview caused more commotion than anything I had ever seen up to this point. From protests to burning Beatles records to some radio stations refusing to air their music. Lennon later apologized at several press conferences, and people just moved on to the next news story. The Beetles had to move on as they had just come out with their newest album, Revolver.

By this time, I was not that big on the Beetles anyway. So many other groups came out during this time that they became just another group, not the phenoms they once were. The Billboard Top 100 songs came out, and the Beetles' Yellow Submarine came in at number 90. I guess John Lennon's comments took more of a toll than people realized at the time.

During Lent on Fridays the school observed the Stations of the Cross. On the walls inside of the church there were 14 stations. Each station had ornate plaque images that were numbered—seven images on each side.

The images were as follows:

1. Jesus is condemned to death
2. Jesus takes up his cross
3. Jesus falls for the first time
4. Jesus meets his mother
5. Simone of Cyrene helps Jesus carry the cross
6. Veronica wipes the face of Jesus
7. Jesus falls for the second time
8. Jesus meets the women of Jerusalem
9. Jesus falls for the third time
10. Jesus is stripped of his garments
11. Jesus nailed to the cross
12. Jesus dies on the cross

13. Jesus is taken down from the cross

14. Jesus laid in the tomb

As the priest and altar boys approach each station, they would genuflect and pray, "We adore you, O Christ, and praise you. Because by your holy cross, you have redeemed the world." Then, they would recite a passage from the Bible describing each station.

It was magical and mysterious, and it felt like we were back in time. The lights were lowered to make it easier to focus on each station. Being a new server and not really a good one, I was not allowed to be one of the altar boys for the Stations. But this was truly the best experience one could have. We sat by grade, with our nuns in each section, all of one mind, with our hearts praying as one. It was the warm embrace of Jesus. I hoped one day I would be chosen for the Stations to be right there on the spot, soaking it all in.

I had a bike that we brought from Warwick. It was old and made for a little kid. There were no gear speeds. I asked mom and dad if I could get a new bike for my birthday but was flatly refused. It cost too much, and my current bike was sufficient. I was heartbroken riding my bike while the other kids had bikes with three speeds. I felt like a little kid on my bike.

I woke up on Easter morning, my birthday. But you already know my birthday is on Easter. As I opened my eyes, I saw a brand new three-speed bike. I couldn't believe my eyes! I was in utter shock. I closed them again, opened them, and the bike was still there. I was not dreaming after all. I screamed and hollered, so everyone came to my room to see the commotion. This has always been my favorite present. I was more than surprised and realized my parents loved me. I knew I often got into trouble, but they still loved me. I would now be able to keep up with the other kids when we ride our bikes, and I would not be ashamed to ride with them.

I was in the choir for about three months until my voice got deeper. It cracked during a song, and they kicked me out. My voice cracked a lot, and Mary gave me a lot of teasing at home. I guess it was payback for the Amazon label I put on her. Dad started calling me Thor because my voice was so deep. Heck, even I was surprised by the way I sounded. When I laughed it sounded like thunder, so they say. You would hear dad yelling from another part of the house, "Shut up, Thor."

My Dad gave me another name, which was more of a phrase. My family still says it to me when I goof up on something. Usually, it is something major. It is 'ONE STEP BEYOND." He would look at me and say, "You're just ONE STEP BEYOND!" I think it was a proper phrase for me. I never knew when to stop teasing or arguing to get my point across.

1966, the St. Louis Cardinals moved from Sportsman's Park to the new Busch Stadium. I started playing in the CYC league. This stood for the Catholic Youth Council. I was to be the number 1 left-handed pitcher.

Okay, I was the only one who could throw the ball over the plate. On the team, the manager was Sister Agnes, and we had 3 nuns as the 1st base coach, 3rd base coach and one as the cheerleader. Nuns in full habits. How in the hell can a guy concentrate with all this pressure!

We were not allowed to stand when not in the batter's box or on deck. They were strict, and we were not allowed to say, "Hey, batta, batta, batta," to make the batter nervous. We could not yell or scream. We had to be polite and be gentlemanly. The nuns were always jumping up and down and getting into the games. I think they had more fun than we did.

We were going into our 3rd game out of 10, and I was warming up. I did not wear my glasses that day because they used to fog up and make me sweat—just another humid day in St. Louis. Without my glasses, I could not see the home plate. I could barely see the catcher's mitt when moving it around. I could not see the catcher's signals on which pitch to throw as I practiced. Because of this, I knew I did not have my stuff. I could not get the ball in the strike zone. I had lost my confidence due to a lack of clear vision. This would be the worst game I ever played, and it would stay with me all these many years.

I went up to talk to the manager, Sister Agnes. I told her I did not have my stuff and needed to be pulled before we started the game. She told me to settle down, and I would be fine. I was not happy with her decision to keep me in the game. I did not throw one strike during the warm-up pitches. I was doomed to fail.

We were the home team, so we took the field first. The first batter I faced, I walked. The second batter attempted to bunt, and I beaned him good for trying to bunt on me. After all, that is what Bob Gibson would do. You do not bunt against Bob! Now we have a man on first and second. I was in trouble big time. I stopped with my windup and went to the stretch for a quicker delivery. I probably should have pitched from the stretch when I had a man on first, but he was overweight and a very slow runner. If he attempted to run, I would pick him off.

Why he was the lead-off hitter confused me, but either way, he was on first. Now we have a man on first and second. Pitching from the stretch, I walk the 3rd batter. I called for time out, walked over to Sister Agnes, and said, "Pull me and pull me now." She looked at me and said, "Calm down, you can do this." The other three nuns are jumping up and down, yelling defense, defense. This is not a football game, Sisters!

You got it! With the bases loaded, I walked the 4th batter, and a run scored. I was so mad at Sister that I called time again. This time, she came out to the mound, and the guy from 3rd base and the catcher came out to discuss what we were going to do. Sister just said, "You are the only one who can pitch the ball. You are it and will not leave this mound until you get three outs. Do You understand me? Now concentrate and strike this batter out!" I had no way out of this mess, and Sister was serious about it. I had to pull myself together. I told the catcher that I could not see his signs for what pitch to throw. He came up with three pitches in the order we needed, and those would be the pitches I'd throw. He was to hold the mitt right over home plate and not move it around. It worked, strike out number one. He came to the mound on the second and third hitter to tell me what pitches to throw for each batter.

I was good to go now and to tell the truth, I do not know if we won that game, but it gave me confidence, keeping me in through all the drama I was causing. Next time, I will wear my glasses no matter what!

I came home with the news that I would be serving the high mass on Sunday at 11 am. It was a big event for me and my family. Of course, dad wanted to sit in the back of the church, and I was happy he was out of my sight. I was under a lot of pressure as it was. We had four altar boys, two on each side of the altar. Being my first time, I figured I would just go through the motions. The older kids told me I would be on the right side facing the altar and would ring the bell. I was not sure when to ring the bell during mass. During the Eucharist, it is rung three times, once before the Words of Institution and once at each elevation of the Host and of the Chalice. We did the triple ring each time. The guy kneeling next to me would ensure I rang the bell. At the right time, he would give me a nudge so I would not screw it up. I could not understand why I had to do this. It was my first time.

My time came to ring the bell. I picked it up and shook the bell, but it did not ring, it just went around it. Just one bell so only one chance to ring. Why did it just go around?

The clapper did not hit the sound bow! At this point, the two altar boys across from us were giggling. The altar boy next to me was frozen stiff. I whispered to him, you do it. He said no way. I was up again, and the guy nudged me to get ready. I shook the bell again, and the same thing happened: no sound, just going around and around. We were all giggling and could not kneel without moving—the third time. I assured myself that I am sure this damn bell will ring. I got the nudge, and I was ready. I swung the bell hard. It went around and around with no sound.

We were giggling so loud and could not kneel still. My dad said he could see us screwing around from the back of the church. He was also happy to be sitting in the back of the church. I was wondering if I was being pranked. Was the bell broken or what?

Father Ellis then put his hand over the microphone and said the same thing to all of us. He looked right and spoke and then left. Words of wisdom flowed from his lips. "Shut up, you little bastards!" We responded," Yes, Father."

It was so hot in the summer, and without air conditioning, dad signed up the family to join a pool in Sunset Hills. He said the one in Crestwood cost too much. We had to drive instead of walking to the pool. We would go three or four times a week, which was a great relief. I ended up having a problem, and I did not know what to do. I asked some guys what they were doing when going to the pool. I had problems in class when I had to stand up, speak, and answer. I had to put a book in front of my pants to hide my boner. It would just happen, and it seems like I was always experiencing it. I mean, from cooties to boners, what is a guy supposed to do? Why was this happening to me?

I walk into dad's room and ask him to buy me a supporter. He said you don't need a supporter. You're too young for that, and you are not playing organized football. I kept asking, and he kept saying no. We went to the pool that night, and I was in the water for over 2 hours. I could not come out. I had a boner, and it was like a rudder when I tried to swim.

Dad called me over to the end of the pool where we were sitting. He looked down at me, "David, we are leaving now. Get out of the pool."

"Dad I can't get out,"

"What? Do you have a leg cramp?"

I looked up right into his eyes, red-faced and whispering. "Do you remember when I said today I needed a supporter?"

He started laughing, and it was so loud. "Dad! It won't stop. I can't get out like this!" He then got a beach towel and came up and held it in front of me. Then, I wrapped it loosely around so I would not show it.

The next day, dad called me to his room and handed me a supporter. I opened it up and said, "How do you put this on?" I was so clueless.

One night, I was working with a new altar boy during the Benediction of the Blessed Sacrament. The priest handed me the Thurible holding the incense. The priest went first, and we followed behind him. I was not trained in what to do. Despite not being trained in what to do, we were standing behind the priest. It was then that the new altar boy whispered and asked me a question.

"Do you use the incense?"

"That is a good question, I guess? He did hand it to me."

"When do you use it?"

I replied, "I guess when the priest kneels or stands. Whenever he moves, I will swing the incense. Makes sense to me."

I was not aware that I was only to hold it for the priest. The service started, and I was standing behind the priest, shaking and waving the incense all over the place. I waived it in three directions, and every time the priest moved, I moved it up and down. This went on for 10 minutes. Suddenly, we were unable to see the priest through the cloud of incense that I was creating. We had no idea where he went. I turned around and could not see anyone in the congregation. It was just a cloud of incense.

At once, out of the cloud, comes the priest. He was so mad his face was red, and he had these huge bulging eyes. Angrily, he yanked the Thurible out of my hands and told us to sit down in the front pew on the other side of the church. After the Benediction, the priest came over to us. He asked if Tony trained us. We shook our heads no, and he said, "You both will never ever hold the Thurible again, do you understand me?" "Yes, Father, we do." We walked away knowing Tony was in deep shit. The bell was at high mass, and now it's no wonder they got me stuck doing the 6 am mass seven days a week. I was like Dirty Harry getting all the crap jobs.

We won a few games in the Khoury League and felt confident. Of course, we only played the worst teams in the league up to this point. We did not have a stellar team by any means. In every game, our manager would be thrown out by the 3rd inning of the game for arguing with the umpire. Mr. George, the sponsor and coach, would then manage the team.

I was a left-hander, our team had a chance to win if I had control. However, our main pitcher, who happened to be the manager's son, threw side arm right-handed and had good control most of the time. He was the main pitcher and good enough to compete with anyone. Unfortunately, our center fielder could not catch a fly balls and choked in every game. Additionally, our right fielder was overweight, which caused him to struggle to hit an obvious home run, and soon would be out of breath getting to second base. He would turn a double into a single. Despite this, he would the best hitter we had. On the bright side, the infield was very good, so we won most of our games. Mr. George worked on the basics with the infield in every practice. I played center field, and occasionally right or first base when I did not pitch.

Chapter 22

Overcoming Fears

Depending on who was pitching we rotated the outfield and first base. No one messed with third, shortstop or second base. They were fantastic and maintained their positions. We had enough utility players to cover every other position. It was fun to play different positions and sometimes in the same game.

Some of the parents would buy soda and snacks for after the game in each game. Most parents purchased Cokes or Pepsi and 7up, but not my parents. They purchased the local brand Vess Soda and generic snacks. I would always hear, "Oh no! It's turn! First, it was burlap sacks, and now this!"

Kids would come up to me and ask why my parents were so cheap. I had no answer for them. I just said they were from Rhode Island.

I was still standing in front of my parents' bedroom mirror, imitating Bob Gibson. I was perfecting my slow, beautiful windup with a scowl on my face.

In one game, my best friend was on the opposing team. He had the same first name as me and was an inch taller. He was strong as an ox, and when he ran, it was like slow motion. He was so slow. He could hard hit the ball and be difficult to catch going through the infield. He was on third, and I was pitching. I was into my beautiful slow wind-up, and the coach on their team told my friend to steal home plate. He had plenty of time to go down the line with me in my beautiful wind-up. That was the last time I had ever done a slow wind-up pitch. He was a very slow runner and stole home on me—Mr. Michelangelo of the wind-up. I was the brunt of jokes for the rest of the season. After that, I just practiced the Bob Gibson scowl.

Johnny and I would go to Crestwood Mall every chance we got. Our idea of fun was to make fun of people or prank them. We would stand outside the big window at Woolworths, where the customers were having meals. Each of us would stand on each end of the window. I would signal, and at the same time, we would stand right in front of the window to catch a diner's eye. When this happened, we took our hand, rubbed our bellies, mouthed I'm hungry, and disappeared to the window's ends. Once, a man was eating with two other men, and he saw us and tapped the guy next to him and pointed at the window, but we were gone. A couple of minutes later, we again did it to him. After the third time, we figured he might come after us, so we had to move on. Ah, great fun we had at the mall.

Another time, a woman was eating right next to the window. I went up to the window, used my hands, and pointed out that my mom knew you. She mouthed hello, and I put my hand on my belly and said I was hungry. She then motions for me to come in and eat. Johnny was laughing on the other side of the window, so I grabbed him and asked if he could also eat. She indicated for us to come in. We acted like we would go in but ran off as fast as we could.

On a different occasion at the mall, an older lady was dressed to the hilt, wearing fox fur. This lady is walking down the center of the mall in heels when Johnny came up behind her. He was barking like a dog walking behind her because she wore fox fur. Other patrons of the mall stopped what they were doing, wondering what this kid was doing to this lady. She picked up her speed, and Johnny quickly followed, barking in tow. Suddenly, she turns around and looks down at him. She barks like a little yappy dog right back at him. She was so awesome at doing this; everyone just bellowed the biggest laughs you ever heard. She got him good in front of everyone. And away she walked with her head held high.

All the boys were jealous in school as the girls were fawning over Davy Jones of the Monkees. How can you compete with this? The TV show was great; every week after the show, the girls would make a big deal out of it. They knew it was driving us crazy, and some girls had boyfriends. They would wear a boy's ID bracelet proudly. I was still in a fog as I had no idea how to talk to girls. I just got over the fact that they no longer have cooties, and I was starting to like girls. I was busy with baseball and being a server and had zero contact with girls outside of classes. We were no longer separated in class, only when we were on the playground.

I did not plan on talking about this, but I guess it needs to be told. I will not explain how it happened or what happened to me to be in this situation. I stuttered so badly I could not even say my last name without stammering. I was unable to complete a sentence on the telephone due to this. It started before I went into the first grade. This was the real reason I never used a phone. I probably should have mentioned this earlier, but I did not intend to tell you about it. I do not have the problem now, so I guess I just blocked it from my memories, and it came rushing back to me. I was facing this when I was five years old.

I needed professional help as I was also sleepwalking. One time, I almost went out the back door of the house. It became necessary for me to get treatment; therefore, I had to see some doctors. My parents said they were special doctors, not the shot kind of doctors. My parents told me to talk to them. They really want to get to know you. I never told my parents why I was having problems. I was sure I would not tell some other grown-up either.

During my visits to the doctors, I had to put blocks of different sizes into holes and time doing it. I had to take the Ink Blot Test. I looked at so many that they started to look the same. There were hearing tests and others as well, all to find out what the problem was. They never got to the source of the problem. No one would ever know. No matter what test they gave me, there was no improvement. The stuttering was embarrassing and caused me to go into a fit of rage and fight for my honor. This was a major reason for most of the fights in school. This is difficult for me to talk about right now. But I am okay now. You will understand why Nuns were my heroes in more ways than one.

Sister announced that she would pick certain students for the St. Louis speech contests planned every year in the Archdiocese. She picked me and a friend of mine. I was horrified that she chose me and became flush with the thought of people laughing at me stuttering. All my prayers each day had a part devoted to this problem.

After the last class of the day, I waited in the classroom. When everyone had left, I went up to talk to Sister Agnes, who was cleaning the blackboard. I asked if she had a minute to talk. I asked her not to use me for the speech contest and said it would be better for the school if I were not a part of it. I can't talk, Sister, you know that. She had me sit at one of the desks and pulled her chair over to me to talk. She and I had a special bond.

"I am doing this for you. I know I can help you overcome this so that you will no longer be afraid of speaking around people. I realize this is a major problem, and you get into trouble because of it. I can see the pain in your face when I call on you."

"But Sister, there is no way I can do this. I do not need people I do not even know laughing at me." I was crying at this point and shaking with fear.

"David, I promise I will help and guide you to accomplish this great feat. We will do this together." Sister helped me with my lines every day, and then, combined with my friend, we had the lines down. By the way, the skit Sister chose for us was "Leave it to Beaver." I played the part of Wally, Beaver's brother. I was a foot taller than my friend, so he played the Beaver. After a few weeks, I stopped stuttering while doing the skit and could perform my part very well.

When we arrived for the contest, Sister gave me a private pep talk and said that she was proud of me no matter what happened. The fact that I worked so hard in her heart made her know I would perform well. This gave me the courage to get out there and talk! We took first place for our grade, which was a big thrill for the school. We had to perform this in front of the whole school next week. I wish I could say my stuttering ended, but it did not. However, it gave me a flicker of hope in knowing that I could talk around people. I remember the training and Sisters' words from that time on. I got a little better each year due to Sister Agnes's faith in me. I will never forget her ever!

I was sitting in the middle of the second row next to Frankie. He had this shit-eating grin on his face. He said, "Watch what I can do?" He drops his pencil on the floor and goes to retrieve it. While he is on his knees, he looks up at this girl's skirt. I was shocked at this. Why would he do something like this? Is he just crazy or what? As he was mesmerized at his sight on his knees, Sister caught him. "Frankie, what are you doing?" Sister was livid. Frankie jumps up, and Sister grabs him. They go over to the wall. As she grabs his head, she is screaming what a devil he is. She is banging his head hard against the cement block wall with both hands. Then, two other nuns who heard her screaming came rushing in, and Sister whispered what Frankie had done.

They threw him out into the hall. All you could hear was the banging of his head and body against the wall. I did not tell anyone what happened. Sister did not tell anyone either. But he was gone for the day after this—three nuns on one. That guy was done.

A few days later, another incident happened in class. Do you remember that kid Kevin when I put him in a bear hug to see if his back would crack? Well, he was a good kid, and we all liked him. He had a good sense of humor and never got into trouble until this one day. He did have one issue. He liked to take the boogers out of his nose and put them under the desktop. We all knew this now, but I figured at least he did not eat them like another person I knew.

Sister sees this and yells, "Kevin, what did I tell you the last time? I made you clean all the undersides of all the desktops!" Hmm, I did not know this. Maybe she has a point. She called him to the front of the class. She pulled out her chair, and in front of everyone, she bent him over her knees and spanked him hard over and over. When she finished, he got up, and his face was so red, but he had no tears. That impressed me. He was humiliated, and we all hated that nun after that. This could have been one of us. It's not the booger part, but something, I'm sure.

He then had to clean the desk during class. No one ever spoke of this again. He was one of us—no teasing, nothing. One kid said he should have disposed of the evidence. But this clown was the one who ate the boogers! What an expert opinion.

Mary and I fought all the time. I was sure it was the curse, but I did not care. She was bossing Joanne and I, and it needed to stop. I told her I was tired of it, and she said you want to fight about it? She was a foot taller than me, and we did some sparing, not real fighting. I gave her a right jab, which broke her glasses right in the middle of the frame. "You're really going to get it this time." She screamed. "This will cost a lot of money to fix. Dad told you over and over not to fight with girls." She pointed her finger at me and told me to leave the room. The last words I heard from her were, "I can't wait until Dad comes home."

When dad got home, he was more than upset. He told me to go and take off my shirt and lay on top of his bed face down. He forgot to shut the door to his bedroom like he always did. He then took a belt and started to whip me on my back. This went on for a while. Mary went by the room and looked in. She started screaming for my dad to stop. Then mom came running down the hallway and started yelling, and finally, dad stopped. He lost control this time. He did this to me before, but the strikes were not as many as these. I could always take it and never told anyone that he beat me on my bare back. To be honest I thought it was a normal thing.

I spent the rest of the night in my room, dreaming about beating him up. This time, I would not take all the blame. Later, Mary said she was sorry, and we never had a problem after this. We became closer and started doing things together. She never realized how the beatings went. If that door were shut, no one would ever have known it was going on. I never yelled or moaned. I would not give my dad the satisfaction.

This opened her eyes, and she kept an eye on me. We started hanging out and listening to her collection of 45s. Mom had no idea that I was getting whipped like this, either. She just thought dad and I were having private father-son talks.

It was the 9 am Sunday mass, and I was working on the rail holding the communion plate. The priest and I walked back and forth in total unison. We were a great team. Then it happened all at once, and everything stopped moving. No breathing, no nothing! I was standing in front of the most beautiful girl I had ever seen. She had her tongue out, waiting to receive the host for holy communion. All I saw were the biggest breasts I had ever seen in person. Looking down, I had the view of a lifetime. I froze and could not think. I jerked the communion plate right into her throat at the same time the priest put the host on her tongue.

She spit out the host, and it went over the rail and about two feet onto the floor. I just looked down at the host and then looked up at the priest. He looked down, then up at me. Did he want me to pick it up? I did not know the correct protocol for this. Finally, he bent down and stood up and ate it. Then we tried it again, and I was so red-faced and hot after this. Embarrassed, I stood still under her chin, but it went okay, and then I went on to the next parishioner.

When mass was over, the other server said, "Well done O'Rielly, you are famous now!" That is when I realized for sure that girls do not have cooties.

Summer vacation was coming up, and we were all handed cards dated June 7th, 1966. The Nuns were still looking out for us outside of school.

Dear Boys and Girls

Have fun this summer, but remember these things:

1. Say your morning and evening prayers every day.
2. Do not do anything you are ashamed to have Mother and Dad know about.
3. Go to mass every Sunday; Confession and Holy Communion at least every two weeks.
4. Be modest and respectful in your dress, especially when visiting the Blessed Sacrament.

5. Treat others as you would like to be treated.

6. August 15th is a Holy Day of Obligation.

7. Go to Mass on first Fridays.

8. Always tell your parents where you are going, with whom, and what time you will return.

9. Cross streets only at intersections where there is a light or Traffic Officer.

10. Wait at least one hour after eating before entering the water. Always swim with a companion and stay close to shore.

****

During 1966, I had several cousins in the armed services, and several went to Vietnam. In Catholic school, we were provided literature about Catholic heroes who died in Vietnam. They would tell their stories of bravery and death. In the vestibule, the church started putting up plaques of fallen soldiers who were members of our church. They were on both sides of the wall by the time the war was over. The sisters would pass out literature of the fallen with stories of bravery and their final sacrifices. That we should rise to the occasion if our time should ever come. We hoped that day would never come. We were scared shitless.

I was in 6th grade and felt like I was back in time at the Bay of Pigs. All the boys were freaking out as this war was not slowing down. There was no end in sight. We knew it would be our time to join up when we came of age. This is when I started to watch the evening news about Vietnam and paid close attention. Our family would watch the Huntley Brinkley Report on NBC. Chet Huntley would be in New York, and David Brinkley in Washington. At the end of the report, they used the same catchphrase. "Good night Chet, and Good night David, and Good night for NBC news." The news ran for 30 minutes, so it held my attention. My future did not look promising. My cousins were on my mind, and I was worried for them.

My mom sent one of my cousins a box of wine and pepper biscotti that he received while on board a ship heading to Vietnam. The sergeant made him eat all the biscotti at once. He wrote a letter to my mom, saying thanks but please do not send food again.

Chapter 23

The Changing and Challenging Times

1967

One of the highlighted events in 1967 was when boxer Muhammad Ali was stripped of his Heavyweight title for refusing to be inducted into the US Army. Everyone I knew was calling him a coward, but I knew differently. I had watched him fight a lot since he beat Sonny Liston. He refused due to his religious beliefs. There were a lot of demonstrations against the war in Vietnam. I was still confused about this, so I started to pay attention to what was happening and why. I watched the news with my parents and asked a lot of questions.

The world was changing all around me. There was more in life happening all over, and my little world was getting trampled and swallowed up. I was getting older and becoming aware. I was too naive to understand things. I grew up way too fast, observing all the changes in the surroundings around me. But I did not know this. The country was on fire, from protesting Vietnam to riots and civil rights protests in major cities. During the Six-Day War, people were of the view that the end of the world was near and often quoted Revelations in the Bible as proof. I

234

could not understand all the craziness. My life's foundation was falling due to the cracking walls of what I had always believed to be true.

The only good thing would have to be when Carl Yastrzemski won baseball's triple crown. Of course, the St. Louis Cardinals defeated the Boston Red Socks to win their 8th World Series Title. By this time, I was solely a St. Louis Cardinal fan. Baseball and the Catholic Church kept me busy and grounded, and I needed this with all that was happening at the time. I was twelve years old and would be a bonafide teenager next year. I was looking forward to not being a kid any longer, being able to drive a car, and experiencing freedom like never before in a few years. I wanted to travel anywhere and see new things. I could not wait to get older and experience freedom. But what freedom really meant, I could not say.

My head was spinning at the thought of being a grownup. I was confused and scared. To a kid, the world was getting bigger, not smaller. Everybody had an opinion on everything from Hard Hats for the war to hippies against the war. Everything was changing around me: hairstyles, clothes, music, and girls.

It was an explosion of new ideas and ways to express yourself. I did not have any money, so I made a peace sign out of the plastic on top of a Maxwell House coffee can. My sister Mary gave me a necklace made out of pieces of plastic to hold the peace sign around my neck. I wore this cheap crap everywhere I went. I was making a statement. I did not

235

know what that statement was, but that is what I told people. I felt I was half establishment and half hippie, in other words, sitting on the fence, unable to make a serious decision.

Speaking of girls, we were having our annual school picnic, which was held in a park with all the rides and booths. Each Catholic school would take a turn at this park. I wanted to ask this one girl out. I was mad about her. I really admired her, but I did not know how to ask her out or even to talk to her. I had zero social skills when it came to girls. I talked to Mary about this, and she said she would help me. I said I was too nervous, so we practiced what to say so I could ask her for her home phone number at school. I would then call her up and talk to her after school.

When I got home, I picked up the phone, but it slipped out of my hand—sweaty hands from the nerves that took over. Mary said I will help you. Put your hand on the mouthpiece, and we will put our heads close to the earpiece to hear her. Mary then told me exactly what to say. The girl probably thought I was hearing impaired because I did not respond quickly when we talked. My sister helped me get a date! I owed her for that one.

It was now time for the talk. Dad should have talked to me two years earlier, as my friends already had an awkward conversation with their fathers. Now, it was my turn. He came into my room with a record player. I told him I knew all about sex with girls, but he said I want you to get it from the right source. He said listen to the record and let me know when you are done. I will come back in when you are finished, and if you have any questions, you can ask me then. The record made me even more confused and contradicted all I knew about girls and sex. I realized my friends did not have a clue either. Dad came again, and I had no questions for him. I could not talk to my dad about sex.

I totally realized that this is why they decided to teach Sex Education in schools. Some things are just too awkward to talk to your parents about. Maybe it would have worked if I had not listened to a recording first. I might have been able to open up, yeah right.

Music was great in 1967. This helped to take the edge off, and I listened to a variety of rock and soul music on my transistor radio. Music changed from Frankie Valli's 'Can't Take My Eyes Off of You,' or The Turtles' 'Happy Together,' to 'White Rabbit' from Jefferson Airplane. Hard Rock was making a play for the airwaves. Soul music also had a ton of variety, like the Four Tops "Standing in the Shadows of Love." 'Soul Man' from Sam and Dave. The Temptations and Supremes ruled the airwaves. With the earpiece, I would listen to late-night Cardinal games while falling asleep. I would always wake up when Harry Carry would scream, "Holy Cow."

We listened to radio station KXOK on the AM dial 630 to hear the radio personality Johnny Rabbit in 1964. His real name was Ron Rlz. Ron left in 1964 but was unable to keep Johnny Rabbitt's name, so a new disc,

237

Jockey Don Pietromonaco, took over as the Rabbit. He played 45s until 1969 when the station retired the name. It was fast and exciting, never boring. But there was more variety in the KXOK selection. They also played Soul music, which was huge in St. Louis. It was the only music you could really feel in your heart and dance to. Having soul music at a dance calmed people down to just swing with the music. KSHE, an FM station, started in 1967 and soon became the premier Rock Station for the St. Louis metro area. It was still going strong today.

Everybody was dancing except for us. You see, we had no real interaction with girls. We were clumsy, goofy oafs who had no clue how to talk to a girl. The nuns in 7th grade decided it was time for us to interact. We were instructed to go downstairs in the basement to the cafeteria. Inside one of the rooms, the girls sat on one side of the room and the boys on the other. We had no idea what was going on. Sister entered the room with a record player and told us to dance. The music was old and slow, meant for generations before us. Nobody moved. We just sat there. Then she paired us up and put us in the middle of the room. She and another sister then showed us how to dance, and they danced around the room. This did not help at all. We were so frozen and awkward, and it took us a few minutes to dance. The girls were just as nervous and awkward as us. I remember my hands were so sweaty I had to wipe them on my pants every minute or so. The nuns would work the room and separate us if we were too close to one another like that was going to happen.

Being in 7th grade meant one more year to go. My grades were decent, but I had to improve to be accepted into a Catholic high school. Taking the entrance exam to get into the school you wanted was not easy. Good grades, good school. Poor grades: you went to public school or if the tuition was too high for the parents to pay. I now had a goal to improve. I stopped with the funny antics in school and hit the books hard. I liked research and finding answers to problems. Except for math and science, I did well.

We were having a baseball game in the city. The field was rough and not well maintained. I was pitching this day on a flat mound. It was rare to see a flat mound on a field we would play on. We were used to pitching off the mound, so flat was awkward, but that is how we started in the league. During the game, things got heated. I had a runner on first base, and he was yelling that I did not have my stuff. It got so bad I called time and went over to talk to him. I simply said to shut up, or I would bean him the next time he was at bat. He shut up fast. Then I looked over to the street behind 3rd base and saw four guys stripping a car. Only in the city did I think about it, and I continued to pitch. About 5 minutes later, the police came up with a paddy wagon to take them away. It was just another CYC game, and we got slaughtered. I guess I did not have my stuff after all.

David Michael O'Rielly

In 1967, we achieved what we had never thought was possible in the Khoury League. Our team was playing the last game of the season, and then we went on to the playoffs for first place. It was hard to believe we had come this far. We played a tough team, and I came in as a relief pitcher. I had to get through three more innings. We only played seven innings in a game.

It was a close game, and I was on fire. I had my stuff, and I could throw hard and accurately. My curveball would go in towards a right-handed hitter and then curve over home plate for the strike. Most of the batters would pull away, thinking the ball would hit them. My finest memory, no doubt. Bob would have been proud.

We came down to the final out. Do you remember me mentioning our center fielder who could not catch a fly ball? Well, we had two outs, and if we get the third out, we will win. I went into my wind-up and threw the ball hard. The batter hit the ball high up into center field. There was a man on third, but he had to wait to see if the ball would be caught.

Crossing the plate does not count for a run if a ball is caught. The stats say you would have been left on base. Plenty of time to run and score if the ball is not caught. The ball was coming down, we all said oh shit! In unison. We knew he would never catch that ball. I watched the ball coming down, and we are all screaming instructions for him to catch the ball. I had never seen a ball hit so high in the air. It took forever to come down towards him.

240

He got underneath it and had his glove in position. He caught the ball! We all ran over to him, picked him up, and carried him to our bench. He was the hero of the day, and this gave him the confidence he needed for the other playoffs. It was like a light switch. We were so proud of him.

Also, can you recall that our team had some issues? The center fielder catching the ball had such an impact on all of us. We could do better, and we could take first place. In two weeks, we would play for the championship. The game was held at a high school, and they had real dugouts. It was intimidating to be on this field. I was to be the starting pitcher. It was a dark, cloudy day. I was ready and eager. I had Bob Gibson burning in my heart and soul. I was ready to be as fierce as Bob. Just call me Bob. I am Bob, and we will win!

My fastball was good and overpowering. I owned the curve and threw in a slider every so often to keep them thinking. Their shortstop tried to bunt to be the first batter to reach base in the third inning. I tried to bean him, but he was fast and agile. It was difficult pitching because he was so short. The strike zone was very small. I ended up walking him, but he never made it to second base. Like I said, I was on fire.

By the middle of the fourth inning, it started to rain, and time was called. We were up by two runs, but they called the game without a winner. You had to have four complete innings to have a winner in case of rain. I was pissed as I was doing well but what about next time? The special umpire said we must decide on a new date, but it must be played to determine who takes first place in our division.

Our manager decided to have a meeting right after the game was called. He said we did really well and appreciated us for coming this far. However, there was a good chance we could lose. His idea was not to play the final game, and both teams would end up in first place. He said some of you will pretend to go on vacation. You will not answer the phone at home if someone calls. I will tell them we can't put a team together due to vacations. There will be two teams tied for the first position. This has never happened before in the league. We knew this was not right but nevertheless, we followed his instructions. It was sneaky, and we justified it with the fact that we were up by two runs, which sure looked like we would win. The damn rain ruined everything.

Our team and parents went to the baseball dinner for the first-place winners for each division. We were all dressed up in suits and were excited. When we were announced for the first time ever, two teams took first place, and the other players in the room booed us. They knew damn well we pulled a fast one. We were booed again when we went up front to receive the trophies. We deserved it, but heck, we each had a 1967 baseball trophy. Sits on one of my bookcases to this day! Boo, that sucker! I think I will polish it right now. I did not have to; it looks great!

We used to have traveling priests come and perform the mass. It was always awkward for them as each church was a little different in how each performed the mass. During the Homily, they would always ask for money for charity. The Irish priests were the best. With a thick Irish brogue, they would prep us before we started. They wanted to know our routine so the mass would run smoothly.

One Irish priest was great. He was older and energetic and joked with us before we started. "Okay boys, let's remember to put on a good show before we go out to the stage." Then he slapped the back of our heads as we went out as a reminder not to screw up. I wondered at the time if he heard about me.

The 5 pm mass on Saturday night was becoming popular so folks could sleep in on Sunday as their obligation was already fulfilled. We were about half full of parishioners, and it looked like I was the only altar boy on duty. I went out to light the candles. I hated this with passion. You use a taper which is a lit wick attached to a long handle. If you are young, it is difficult to light the candles due to your height. You would always have one that was hard to light due to a short wick. Then, 5 minutes before we started, the other altar boy showed up. He was in panic mode. He forgot he had to serve and was at the mall. The problem was this: he was wearing shorts and tennis shoes. I used to call them sneakers, but they were tennis shoes in St. Louis. This was a huge problem, and we had to cover his feet. He had to wear an extra-long cassock to hide his shoes. During the mass, he probably dusted the place.

It would be his job to walk up the steps of the altar carrying the lavabo and pitcher and a towel for the priest to dry his hands. While the priest washed his hands, he recited, "I will wash my hands in innocence so that I will compass thine altar, O Lord."

He carried it up and stepped on the cassock on the second step, but he couldn't go any further, or he would fall. He looked down at me, and I just shrugged. Like, what do you want me to do about it? The priest was waiting and getting impatient. The other altar boy whispers down to me, "I am stuck; I can't move. Get up here and take this from me." Of course, I snicker, get up, take it from him, and pour the water over the priests' hands. The priest gives us a look like what the hell is going on. Then, I had to help the altar boy down the steps so he would not fall. Father had no idea why this was going on and never asked. It was the 5 o'clock mass, and things were casual.

Chapter 24

A Terrible Injury

As usual, I was having problems with dad and school. I was getting into trouble with my big mouth, making comments that should have been kept to myself. I was upsetting everyone around me. Dad said that he and I would go to confession on Saturday. Maybe this would set me right. We both waited in line. I was in line for Father Bob who was the new young priest of the parish. Dad was in line for Father Ellis. Dad went first and made his confession. He came out and told me to get in line for Father Ellis. I objected and said no, I want to talk to Father Bob. Dad pulled rank on me, so I confessed my weekly sins to Father Ellis. I'm sure he remembered I was one of the "Shut up, you little bastards!"

"Are these all your sins that you need to confess?"

"Yes, Father, all my sins."

"Well, this is not what your father told me. Now tell me everything you have done right now."

Busted big time! I had no way out! I was trapped in the confessional with the great inquisitor, Father Ellis. I felt like I was in a medieval inquisition being investigated for heresy. It's just Satan's seed twice removed. What happened to the confidential part?

245

David Michael O'Rielly

I had a friend up the street who was three years older. He was over 6ft and in great shape. His name was Gary, and they moved in around 1965 from Kentucky. He was a good teacher of life, and I looked up to him. We had a lot in common with our dads, but his father was worse than mine. He did not get the belt but was slapped across and punched in the face now and then. We had one thing in common: we liked to walk the railroad tracks into the next town and hang out at the train station. We would get pamphlets and imagine getting on a train and going to a new state. We always talked about running away.

One time, we got on the back of the caboose. I looked in the window, and a crew member caught me looking in. He came after us as we ran down the tracks. There were a lot of workers on the tracks, and this was unusual. He caught us and made us walk back to the terminal. The terminal manager sat us in his office and wanted to know what we were doing. They had seen us plenty of times, and we were now suspects of a train derailment that had occurred earlier in the day. They had witnesses of kids that derailed a train, and he insinuated that it was us. We denied everything and would never ever even consider such a thing. Eventually, we convinced him that we were innocent; we just like walking on the tracks and looking at trains. We were train guys, hello? Gary and I hung out a lot together and listened to soul music. We did not listen to much rock and roll as it changed into hard rock and was difficult to dance to. Like I knew how to dance, right?

One day, Gary was in his room and said, "Do you want to see something? But you can't tell anyone about it. I mean nobody, not even your friends at school."

"Okay sure," I said. I was mesmerized and wondered what he would show me. He slowly checked the door to see if anyone was near his room. He then locked his door and walked over to the closet. He pulled out a box and opened it up, and there were at least 15 Playboy magazines. I heard about them but had never seen one before. It was the holy grail of porn.

Gary said he even reads the articles because they talked about sex and stuff. I never got past the pictures myself. In a few weeks, I eventually reviewed and critiqued every one of them. Of course, what the hell did I know? I had nothing to compare them with.

I learned basic dance moves by watching American Bandstand Playing top 40 hits. They had some variety in the music format but mostly light rock and roll and some soul music. I did not get my smooth dance moves until I started watching Soul Train but that started in 1971. Until then I looked like a spastic stick boy.

In 1967, St. Louis received an expansion hockey team. One more sport to watch which turned out to be good since the St. Louis Hawks moved to Atlanta in 1968. My cousin Steven in Providence played hockey, but it turns out I did not have the ability. I had zero balance and weak ankles. I was not too upset since baseball was my number one sport.

If you recall, we did not have tornado warnings until a tornado hit in 1967. Since we did not have a basement, we would ask to go next door to their basement or to a house up the street. On January 24^{th,} an F4 tornado hit and ripped a 21-mile path of destruction in South County, where we lived. It was terrifying, to say the least. It hit areas to the north and east of us. We thought hurricanes were bad, but with a tornado, you never know where or when it would strike. We held a family meeting to become more prepared and asked many questions with the family we were hunkered down with.

Chapter 25

The Turning Point

1968

Being in 8th grade meant I had no one to worry about. I could handle myself on my own. I ensured that if there were a fight, it would be with me first. I broke up a lot of fights. But I did have a big relapse. I became a jerk, and it took me a while to realize this. I was teasing another boy like everyone else. He had a medical condition, and he had a foul odor. He could not run very well, and we would take his ball cap and play keep-away. He was happy thinking we were playing with him, but we were not. We were cruel and vicious with him.

Suddenly, as if God slapped me on the left side of my head, I got an awakening. A voice in my head screamed out, "What are you doing teasing this boy who has problems? You should be taking care of him. Not tormenting him!" I then pushed some of the guys back, retrieved his hat from them, and put it on his head. This was the only time anyone ever played with him, and he did not understand why I stepped in. I could feel his joy, but this was at his expense.

I went to all the tormentors and told each of them the same thing. "I was wrong in teasing him. We have all been wrong. Not his fault he has problems, and this stops now!" I told them that he would hang out with us from then on. No more teasing. He became part of our group and hung out with us every day—this kid made me a better person by opening my heart. I finally learned compassion and empathy. I realized it was not all about me; we had to take care of others. I found out he died a year later due to his illness. I had a difficult time with that. I still do, to tell the truth.

Moving on, we were throwing a football down at Crestwood Elementary and ran into a group of kids. We decided to have a football game. A call went out, and we knocked on some doors to get other kids to play. We returned to play the game with enough kids to play a decent game of full tackle without pads and helmets. It was just another Saturday of pick-up football. We did not have a full roster for a real game, but it did not matter. In our minds, we were the St. Louis Football Cardinals. We were here to play and see if we could beat these kids from another neighborhood.

Not much happened in the first quarter. None of us were really that good to begin with. Most of us were into baseball, not football. But today, it was football. I was running with the football, and a kid came down low to take me out. I turned to get around him, but my foot stayed where it was. He had a firm grip on my leg as I tried to twist away from him. I could score and knew it. I fell to the ground, and the next thing I realize is that I was in a lot of pain, and I couldn't get up. I was moaning, and my right leg did not feel like a part of me. It was a pulsating pain like I had never felt before. Two guys came over from the other team to help stand me up, but I fell right back down. My right leg just gave out. Then I hear someone shout out. "This guy is hurt bad, and the game is now over." We need to get him to his house immediately.

Two guys from the other team walked me home, one on each side holding me up. My friends did not want to go to my house to face my dad. I did not want to face my dad. I knew he would be pissed off as now I would have to go to the doctor. We came up the driveway, and my dad said, "Okay, real funny. I don't buy this fake injury. Let him stand up on his own, and let me see this fake injury." They released me, and I fell right down the driveway. It hurt like hell on the concrete. I was almost in tears and wished I was all alone so I could cry and release the fear I had in me. I knew the injury was serious. It had to be like the Joe Namath knee injury when he went down in a game in 1965. This was major, and my knee was swelling up severely. The kids who brought me into the house left abruptly after hearing the stories about my dad.

It was Saturday, so there was no doctor till Monday. We just put ice on it, and I took some aspirin. Mom was upset that this happened and that I was playing football. She mentioned that I broke my nose playing baseball a couple of years earlier. I was becoming a financial drain. I lay on the couch while they went out to discuss what to do. Meanwhile, my knee was getting bigger and bigger. It was so big I wondered if it would pop and explode.

Mom called the school on Monday to say I would not attend. Joanne would bring my schoolwork home so I could do it, and she would return it to school the next day. I can't catch a freaking break. I felt terrible, and I still had to do the schoolwork. We went to the doctor's office, but he said nothing could be done until the swelling went down. It was several days later when we went back to the doctor. He examined me and said I needed to see a specialist. I thought dad's eyes would pop out at the thought of more money going out. He told my dad to get me crutches, and dad acted like they were made of gold. All I heard on the way home was, "Damn kid." I was still in a lot of pain, but what are you going to do? You suck it up, that's what.

A whole week had now gone by. Dad took me to a doctor who was a physician for the St. Louis Baseball Cardinals. I thought that was cool, but dad did not. All he would talk about was the money it would take to fix the knee. The x-rays showed I had a torn cartilage and ligament. He said my knee was way worse than Joe Namath had. He asked if I wanted to repair the same way Joe's knee was done. It was a special procedure that would make the knee almost like new. He said this would be a good idea if you are good at football and like to play. I looked at my dad, who was as white as a sheet. If I said yes to do it, then he would have to. The panicked look on his face made me start to think. We can't spend the money.

There is no getting around it. He would be on the spot to do the right thing. The easy answer for me was no. I was not that good at football and had no interest in playing in high school and doing what I could without the special surgery. I did not think this would affect my pitching or playing outfield. That's a big mistake right there. My dad's color came back to his face with a sigh of relief. I was to have the procedure done at St. Mary's Hospital. Now I was scared.

As I was being prepared for surgery, I had no idea what to expect from the surgery. I was told that they would shave my knee and the surrounding area. I would be given a shot to knock me out. While on the hospital bed heading towards the operating room, the nurse asked which knee needed the operation. I said, my right knee. Then I questioned myself, hoping they would not operate on the wrong knee. I was panicking, and all drugged up. I had been in the hospital many times for stitches and other minor treatments, but this was the real deal.

I woke up in the recovery room in more pain than I had ever experienced in my life. I was asking for another shot for the pain—no such luck. I had to bear the pain, and I was losing that battle with the nurse. I had never felt this helpless before, and I had no idea what was to happen next. Eventually, I was shifted to my room and had a roommate. He was a gruff man around 45 years old. I was given another shot, and my roommate said just drift off and never land. He laughed and said I will see you when you wake up. Who is this guy?

In the middle of the night, I awoke to a screaming man from down the hall who was out of his mind. He kept yelling for someone and would not shut up. He was in pain and obviously delusional. My roommate Bill said he does this every night. Bill was a mean bastard as he was a racist. He made several comments about African Americans and was of the view that they should all die. Martin Luther King was assassinated on April 4th, 1968, and my birthday was on April 10th. I was 14 years old, hearing all his garbage. He talked about the assassination and that it was a righteous kill. He made comments about the nurses because of their skin color. Now, I did not fully understand all this, and it made no sense to me. Yes, I remembered the riots and seeing the fire hoses and dogs, and I felt things had to change. On TV, as a family, we watched the violence at the 1968 Democratic Convention. Fire hoses were used to knock people down on the street. Then the police showed up with Billy Clubs cracking heads and arms. I did not understand the violence in the cities. I may have been only 14 years old, but I knew better.

Racist comments hurt no matter which side was talking. This was contrary to the teachings in school and church. I believed in total freedom, and now hate was devouring our country. I was not blind or dumb. I was well aware. Why was this man so full of hate? He did not even know the people he was talking about. I just lay still with Sam and Dave's music, 'Soul Man' playing in my head.

This guy was scaring the shit out of me. I had never heard anyone ever talk like this. He was a true bona fide racist. I heard of them but had never met anyone with this much hate. He was evil, and I knew it. He would raise his head and scowl, spewing all this nonsense. There was no love or compassion in his miserable soul. Why am I in this room with him? I drifted in and out of reality due to the drugs and the dark emotional feeling of hate. Was all this really happening? It was worse than the book 'To Kill a Mockingbird.'

The next morning, Bill started up again with his view of the world. He went into detail about his hero, James Earl Ray, who lived just across the river in Alton, Illinois. He talked about how he did it and had friends help him. He said he knew all about it. He knew the people who surrounded James Earl Ray's orbit. This wacko was driving me crazy. I wondered, Who is he? But he was an adult, and I did not know who to talk to and how to get another room. I was too doped up at the time.

I was relieved when I started to receive visitors, but I was still loopy. I would drift in and out of reality. It seemed Bill was trying to convince me to believe in what he believed. This is all he talked about. With this and the yelling every night, I could not wait to go home. I was a character in a horror movie.

Finally, I was able to leave and go home, but first I had to see the Doctor. He reviewed his work and gave me specific instructions on how to strengthen the knee. I had to work on both knees with the exercises. I had to have a rope tied to a 10-pound weight, sit on the edge of a table, and lift each knee separately from the ground to the table. I was prescribed to perform at least 15 reps at a time, three times a day, exercising both knees, which took a lot of time. He told me to keep my leg as straight as possible, and he would see me again in a few weeks.

When I returned to the doctor, my knee was bent. I was unable to keep it straight. The doctor leaned back in his chair and shouted, "I told you to keep this knee straight! Now we have a problem! Do you not listen?"

He had me sit on his couch, grabbed my knee, and pushed the knee down with his forearm to make it straight. The pain was more than I could bear, and I yelled out with tears in my eyes. He laughed and said, "What's the matter, Mary? Did that hurt too much?" I had longer hair than most young men, so he called me Mary. What a prick was the first thing that came to mind. "You want a bullet to bite on Mary?" That pissed me off, and I told him no, I do not need it, and I did not yell again while he was forcing my knee straight over and over again. I would not give him that satisfaction. I was at his mercy, and no mercy was given to me.

After this so-called rehab, he had my dad come into his office. The doctor sat behind his desk. I was sitting in front of him, with my dad standing off to the side. "Your son will not be able to run again; the knee is not stable, and it will not support him. There will be times he will step off a curb and fall." I did not realize that it was this bad. I figured maybe not running fast, but there was no way I would not run. I knew I would be okay, and this would not be permanent. It just couldn't be.

The doctor leaned back in his chair and said, "This will keep David from going to Vietnam." I looked up with a surprised look and just yelled out, "That is the best news I have heard all day!" After all, the war had been going on for years with no end in sight.

The Doctor looked at me with a look of horror. "What is this, you say? Don't you believe in fighting for your country? Do you have pride in being an American?" I only had one thought. What can of worms did I just open? I got good news, and now I am a traitor to my country! The doctor looks over at my dad and says, "Mr. O'Rielly, you fought in WW2, correct?" My dad just shook his head yes. "You understand patriotism and need to teach David here what this means." I thought, you mean Mary, don't you prick? My dad and I left with our tails between our legs. We were defeated and worthless.

When we got into the elevator, I looked up at dad and spoke, "Oh, you fought in WW2, did you? You were a Coast Guard watcher." Dad looked at me, still shocked by what the doctor said. In a way, dad got it worse than I did. He did his service. Not glamorous, but necessary. I realized that I had hurt him with my words, and this made me feel small.

In 1968, I was playing the final year in the Khoury League and CYC. My knee had healed, and my mobility improved. In the first game, I pitched three innings, and then it happened. My knee gave out during the wind-up when my right leg hit the ground, causing me to fall face-first into the ground. From that point on, I could no longer pitch again unless there was a flat mound. I ended up playing center field for the rest of the season. I was heartbroken, to say the least.

I could not put much weight on my right leg, so hitting became difficult. I was done and had just finished out the season. This also meant I could not play high school baseball, which was my dream. In 1967, I went to a baseball camp for pitching and did extremely well. It was expected of me that I would play in high school. Now, what was I going to do?

I was shattered and depressed. When we played pick-up ball, I was now just average. I could not run fast enough to steal a base: no baseball, no football, no nothing I went into a deep depression, feeling sorry for myself. I did not get relief until we went back to Rhode Island.

Steven took care of me, and we hung out at Scarborough Beach every day. We would eat fast food, such as Italian, a loaf of bread and a pepperoni stick. At the beach, there were no fast food chains were allowed, so this was our go-to. There was a store across the street opposite the beach, where we would spend our days for lunch and in the evening.

Steven was like an older brother; we hung out with his friends. Sports was not a big thing with them. It was music and girls. I thought Okay, time to move on. He was also in a band and had a following of girls everywhere he went. He was a local celebrity at Scarborough beach, but it never went to his head.

When we went to Providence, he and I would go collect rent payments. His father owned a lot of rental units in the city. We ran into a lot of colorful characters. We would go with my uncle in his TV repair van and deliver TVs all over the city. This took my mind off my troubles. I was really missing Rhode Island and wanted to move back home and stay with them. I figured dad would be elated if I left, but I could not leave my mom and sisters deep down. I felt they needed me. But I could dream, right?

Steven and his friends were always discussing Vietnam and a senator from Minnesota, Eugene McCarthy. He was anti-war, and everyone I encountered in Providence or Scarborough was talking about him. Four or five guys always slept over at the beach house, and all the conversations revolved around these two topics. Looking back, it makes sense. They were 2 to 4 years older than me, facing the Draft head-on. I became perfectly content with being the age I was.

259

Chapter 26:
Remarkable Years

1969

I was ecstatic when I found out I passed the 8th grade exam and an entrance exam to enter a Catholic boys' school. My hard work in school paid off, and let's face it, I would not have been able to accomplish this great feat without the nun's guidance and persistence.

We went to Mr. Lombardo's house, my dad's direct boss, some weeks later. As I mentioned earlier, two of the bosses transferred with us from Rhode Island, and we knew their families well.

We went outside with a bag of golf clubs. Mr. Lombardo said my knee would get stronger if I played and walked the course. "What do you think, Mary? Does that sound good to you?" This smirking Mr. Prick. He called me Mary, like the doctor, and made fun of my hair.

He started cracking jokes about my long hair, suggesting I should get it cut so guys do not whistle at me. Dad could not say a word, and it was his boss. Good thing I did not have it in a ponytail. He might have made a pass at me. He took out several clubs, and I learned how to hold the shaft and take some practice swings. Mary does not like golf.

Nuns With Nightsticks

Our grade was going to take a trip, and the eighth grade would take a graduation trip. We decided to go to Jefferson City, the state capital of Missouri. Of course, the nuns on our bus had the girls sit up front, and we sat in the back. We toured the State building and then had some free time.

Two guys and I went into an outside magazine stand. I had some money to spend, so I purchased my very own Playboy Magazine. I was an instant celebrity with all the boys sitting in the back of the bus. I hid the magazine under my shirt and tucked part of it into the back of my pants. I thought of charging each guy a quarter to take a peek but was too scared to get caught. A rite of passage, one would say.

All around St. Louis, it was music and dancing. They had grade school dances that high school kids would attend. Many schools would have a dance on Friday nights for 75 cents admission. This was in addition to the closed dances at some of the high schools, and only their students could attend. Some high schools were open to anybody. You could go to any the grade school dances and meet new people. So, my first dance would be at St. Elizabeth's in the parking lot at the back of the school. Most of the school dances had live music. Sometimes, there was just a record player playing 45s. I was pumped up—my first real dance. I was fourteen years old and considered myself to be a hippie. I wore a wide-brim hat, a vest that my mom made for me, and a tie without a shirt. I also wore a plastic peace sign, and my belt was a rope holding up my bell-bottom jeans with the knot to my left side. To top off this ensemble, I wore Jesus sandals. My mom sewed a wild pattern on the sides of my jeans. They were like Civil War pants, the lines going straight down on the sides, but in psychedelic colors.

I was a perfect example of WTF! Looking back, I realize that maybe I should have just worn a burlap sack. I looked like a freak or a bad poster child for the hippies in Haight-Ashbury in San Francisco. I felt cool walking around. When I went to the mall I thought, people stared at me because I did, in fact, looked cool. I now realize that this was not the case. Instead of a rock band, they had a soul band, so I was a little out of place with my cool duds.

The priest, Father William, would monitor all activity at the dance. He was over 6 feet with the body of a linebacker— not someone you would mess with. Father was gentle and good for the kids. He never got angry or yelled, and he had a mellow personality. You could talk to him about anything. Good at confession, not like Father Ryan, the great inquisitor.

A group of boys and a friend of mine came up to me. The leader was small in height but stocky. They surrounded us, and the leader looked at me and said, "I don't like your hippie hat." I looked back at him with a smart-ass look.

"I don't like your face," I replied.

Where in the hell did that come from? Am I just that stupid? So, this guy was looking at his friends, laughing and moving his arms around, getting loose, and talking crap at me.

"Get a load of this guy. Who does he think he is?"

At this point, I realized I should not have said, "I don't like your face" I was way in over my head and heading into the world of deep shit. I was outnumbered, and they were older than me. Why did I wear this stupid hat and sandals? How can you fight with those on your feet? I was analyzing all the different scenarios on how I would get my ass kicked. It did not look good for me.

"You think you're a tough guy, huh? You want to show me what you got?" He was right in my face. I thought I ain't got shit. He was ready to make the first move. I braced myself to hit the guy on my left and move out of the way to miss his punch. I would then have some room to back up and take him down with my wrestling moves.

Out of nowhere, here comes Father William. He got right in the middle of the group, grabbing the front of the leader's shirt and picking him up high in the air, at least a foot off the ground. He said to him, "This young man and his friend go to this school and church, and you do not. I want you to leave these grounds. You will stay here until the boys leave."

Father looked at me and saw Gary standing close by. Gary, luckily, was there for me. He told Gary to take me home now. By this time, my friend had split faster than a road runner.

Father said he would keep the boys right in front of him until he saw I was out of sight. I had never seen Father like this before. No one had, and it shocked everyone. Who would have thought a priest could be that tough and a hero to boot? I already knew the nuns were tough as nails, but not the priest.

Gary and I walked home in a relief that you could not imagine. Father William saved me from getting my ass seriously kicked. Gary said I know those guys from school, and they are tough and pick fights every weekend. They are well known to gang up on you. They do not have a one-on-one fight ever.

Later that year, that leader kid followed a car with a man, his wife, and his mother inside. It was road rage, and he followed them home. On the steps of the guy's home, the leader beat him and stomped him to death. He ended up in prison, not reform school. He was older than I thought. After this, I decided to throw my peace sign in the trash. It was a magnate for idiots like this guy. I was not old enough to talk the talk or walk the walk. I felt like a little kid again, small and fragile in a crazy, mixed-up world. First, Bill was in the hospital, and now this guy. I had to prepare myself. I worked out more with the weights and shadow-boxed to get the rhythm I desperately needed to defend myself. High

School was near at hand. I realized I am not the big fish in school anymore. It starts all over again.

If you think about 1969 and being a 14-year-old, my life was overwhelming. There was so much going on in the world that it was difficult to imagine having a future. I often wondered what my life would be like after I turned 18 and became an adult.

In January 1968, Vietnam was again in the main news. It was the beginning of the Khe Sanh battle near the DMZ. Then, on January 30th, the North Vietnamese launched the Tet Offensive. I had no idea where my cousins were and often wondered.

North Korea seized the USS Pueblo, and the country was at odds over the captain's choice to surrender his light cargo ship, which was used as a spy ship. No Navy captain had ever surrendered before. The captain did the right thing. They could not defend themselves.

Martin Luther King was assassinated On April 4th, 1968, and in June, Robert Kennedy won the California primary and was assassinated. All the angst and fears came back to me in wave upon wave of depression, thinking about John Kennedy.

Vietnam again came front and center with the assignation of a Viet Cong officer by a National Police Chief. This had a much greater impact, as it was shown right in our faces on TV. How could we be righteous in this war? This converted more people to the antiwar movement than anything else.

Demonstrations against the war and Civil Rights became commonplace. Our country was divided, and no one had answers, only beliefs in one camp or another. I was not old enough to make a difference, but I did voice my concerns as it seemed common sense was lacking in grownups. I could not understand if you knew you were heading in the wrong direction to stop, take note, and move in another direction. It made perfect sense to me. But it seemed everyone was in their own trenches, thinking they were fighting the good fight. In 1969, it was like a rush of a violent wind striking me in the face. I was thinking, what's the point?

The only reason I had any common sense was that the nuns in school molded me and taught me right from wrong and how to pray and be one with God. Again, I turned to the guidance and teachings of the Catholic School and Church. I was taught the foundations and meanings of living a good life under God. I finally understood why the school was so strict and structured. It was a teaching moment for all the kids so they could fall back on those times to enable them to make good decisions as adults.

I was now at the age of learning to be a grown-up. Unfortunately, all around me was violence. I carried a non-legal knife that I taped to my leg under my jeans. In my back pocket was a 6-inch folding knife. I never wore shorts in case I had to fight. Hard shoes were best for kicking but slick on the pavement and were still better than sneakers. I was going into High School, so I had to be prepared. I really thought life would be easier as I got older. Having more freedom meant more choices, good and bad. Consequences were something I had to learn about.

I will give you an idea about the idiots in my area. Once, Johnny and I were walking in the Famous Barr parking lot on the way home. It was about 9 pm, so our time out ended. A station wagon loaded with kids comes towards us. They were playing chicken with us and expected us to jump out of the way. They picked up speed, and Johnny ran off to a safe area. But I was stupid and figured they would for sure veer off so they would not hit me with a car. My mistake right there. Big car, steel, and my skinny body. Guess who wins?

They did not veer off, and I had to jump to the left. I put my hand on the hood over the headlight and swung over as the car passed by. It was a loud thump, and they took off, thinking they ran me over. Bastards did not even stop to see if I was alright. I pulled out my knife and yelled for them to stop. Johnny was mad that I did not run off. I heard him all the way home. He was right; I just listened. I was happy my knee did not give out. That was one blessing right there.

It was the beginning of summer, and soon I was going to be a freshman in high school.

I was physically in good shape, even with my weak knee. I was prepared to enter a new world with all new people. I wondered what high school would be like. I was open to anything at this point. This was a chance to test my metal, as they say. I was heading for a new adventure and was up and ready for the challenge.

At this time, I was receiving an allowance of 75 cents per week for chores around the house. Not much you can do with 75 cents, even in 1969. It was time for me to get a real job and earn my own money.

My first job was at the Hong Kong restaurant on Route 66. I was only fourteen so the owner paid me less than minimum wage. I did not have any idea, but it was a job washing dishes. The minimum wage in 1969 was 1.30 per hour, and I received 1.00.

This was one crazy place. As kitchen workers, we were only allowed to eat rice and put chicken sauce on top, which was great. The parents of the owner/ manager sat at a card table day and night on the other end of the kitchen. They would yell obscenities at us in Chinese, and we would yell back our own in English. I worked the evening ship with an older guy out of high school: pots and pans, pots and pans in my dreams, my soapy hands.

A few weeks later, we got into a shouting match with the grandparents on a Saturday night. It was out of hand, and the manager came back and told us to shut up in Chinese and English. Customers were complaining about the noise. I got fired because of this—new guy goodbye.

My next job was working at Baskin-Robbins at the Crestwood Mall. This turned out to be a nightmare. Are you kidding me, 31 flavors? Customers would come up to the counter and sometimes get two scoops of different flavors. The problem was, where were they? I could never find them. I had to have the customers help me and point out which tub of ice cream they wanted. I was in a maze of confusion.

I realized I did not know how to make a change! I had to use a pencil and a pad of paper. I was so nervous about making a change that I just dumped it in their hands. And to make matters worse, your hands would get calluses on a busy day of scooping. Who would think this job would be so difficult? And to top it off, one day, a lady complained that my scoop on her cone was not big enough.

She was yelling at me. "What did I do?"

I said it was the scoop's fault and held it up. When my shift was over, I quit and thought, "forget about it."

My third job was at the Flaming Pit restaurant located on Route 66. It opened in 1964, a well-established place to get a good steak at a reasonable price. This restaurant had a big open charcoal hearth with hickory charcoal broiled steaks.

It had an old-west setting for families and gatherings. When you walked in the front doors, there was an old sea chest replica filled with children's toys; each child could pick one. Kids begged their parents to come to the Flaming Pit.

Keep in mind that the highway going west to east went right through into the city and was slowly driving through each municipality. So you would see two Flaming Pits before you entered downtown.

I started out as a busboy, one of four working on the weekends. During the week, only two or three would work. Most of the guys I worked with were lazy and slow. They did not like working. They would schedule two or three days a week. I put in for six days a week and got it. On the other hand, I learned how to work and the importance of work from my parents. In a month, they laid off all the busboys but three of us. I became the head busboy.

I bussed tables and refilled the two salad bars. I was never standing around. The waitress loved me because I never complained and worked fast cleaning the table and setting it up.

The tables turned quickly, and they made more money, and I got more tips from each of them. We had fun and a lot of laughs.

One time, a waitress bent over at the waitress station, and a guy saw her and was mesmerized. His wife looked over and screamed for the manager. She wanted the waitress fired on the spot because she was not wearing any underwear. She said I will not come back to this restaurant again. The manager apologized and fired the waitress on the spot. When the customer left, he rehired the waitress, but she had to start wearing underwear.

There was an older waitress, and she and I became friends. One night, she was very upset, and the other waitress laughed at her. I went up to her and asked her what was wrong. She said she was at the Steinberg Ice Skating Rink in Forest Park. She fell down, and her wig fell off, and when she stopped sliding, the wig was five feet away from her. I replied that it was no big deal. She said, "No big deal? Someone took a photo of this." She unfolded a newspaper photo that was in the St. Louis Dispatch! I chuckled and said it would be forgotten soon.

A few months later, my waitress buddy approached me and said she did not want to attend he daughter's wedding in California. I, of course, asked why not. She took out the wedding announcement card and handed it to me. The couple on the front were naked, and inside, it stated that it was to be a nudist wedding and clothes were not allowed. I said you can always wear your wig. That's not a funny thing to say, but she was not going regardless.

This turned out to be my job all through high school, and I found my job skills working as a busboy.

David Michael O'Rielly

Well, that's about it. My next venture will be going to a Catholic high school for all boys. All I can say is that the nuns had a significant influence on my life, and I realize it more now as I finish this book. Nun's with nightsticks rock!

You know what's funny? The next nine years were nothing short of unbelievable. Being too literal will be the death of me yet. Wait till we talk again—I have some stories to tell you!

David Michael O'Rielly

Made in the USA
Monee, IL
17 June 2024

477dff80-49e8-4abd-9070-0a69a8c04089R01

.